Great War Literature

NOTES

Written by W Lawrance

on

A Long Long Way

A Novel by Sebastian Barry

Great War Literature Notes on A Long Long Way, a novel by Sebastian Barry.
Written by W Lawrance

Published by:
Great War Literature Publishing LLP
Forum House, Stirling Road, Chichester, PO19 7DN
Web site: *www.greatwarliterature.co.uk*
E-Mail: *admin@greatwarliterature.co.uk*

Produced in Great Britain

First Published 2008.
This Edition published 2014. Copyright ©2005-2014 Wendy Lawrance.
The moral right of the author has been asserted.

ISBN 978-1910603086 Paperback Edition 2
Replaces earlier edition: 978-1905378432

10 9 8 7 6 5 4 3 2 1

Design and production by Great War Literature Publishing LLP
Typeset in Neue Helvetica, ITC Berkeley Old Style and Trajan Pro

Great War Literature Notes on

A Long Long Way

CONTENTS

Preface

Great War Literature Study Guides' primary purpose is to provide in-depth analysis of First World War literature for A-Level students.

There are plenty of other study guides available and while these make every effort to help with the analysis of war literature, they do so from a more general overview perspective.

Great War Literature Publishing have taken the positive decision to produce a more detailed and in-depth interpretation of selected works for students. We also actively promote the publication of our works in an electronic format via the Internet to give the broadest possible access.

Our publications can be used in isolation or in collaboration with other study guides. It is our aim to provide assistance with your understanding of First World War literature, not to provide the answers to specific questions. This approach offers the resources that allow the student the freedom to reach their own conclusions and express an independent viewpoint.

Great War Literature Study Guides can include elements such as biographical detail, historical significance, character assessment, synopsis of text, and analysis of poetry and themes.

The structure of Great War Literature Study Guides allows the reader to delve into a required section easily without the need to read from beginning to end. This is especially true of our e-Books.

The Great War Literature Study Guides have been thoroughly researched and are the result of over 30 years of experience of studying this particular genre.

Students must remember that studying literature is not about being right or wrong, it is entirely a matter of opinion. The secret to success is developing the ability to form these opinions and to deliver them succinctly and reinforce them with quotes and clear references from the text.

Great War Literature Study Guides help to extend your knowledge of First World War literature and offer clear definitions and guidance to enhance your studying. Our clear and simple layouts make the guides easy to access and understand.

The Great War Literature A-Level Study Guide on *A Long Long Way*, provides a critical assessment of many aspects of this novel and is based entirely on the opinion of the author of this guide.

INTRODUCTION

This novel was originally published in 2005 and was shortlisted for the Man Booker Prize that year. It has met with almost universal acclaim and enthusiastic reviews ever since. There are, however, those who find the story in some way lacking, but these are the exceptions rather than the rule.

In this study guide, I have chosen, deliberately, to be one of the exceptions. That is to say that what I have provided here is a critical assessment, giving my opinion of this novel. One of the reasons for this is that to provide another fulsome evaluation would be of little use to students who are trying to compare this piece with others within the genre, simply because there are plenty of reviews which can provide such warm approval already.

Despite the praise which this novel has received, it is certainly flawed and it is these flaws which I have attempted to expose and explore within this guide. Its greatest fault lies in the fact that it is not long enough. The author has such a great talent for language that one wants to know more and yet so much of the war and the events in Ireland have been included that it lacks the detail which is required to really absorb the reader.

That said, A Long Long Way serves a very useful purpose for study. The language is certainly different, as is the political perspective and as such, this book provides some good material for comparisons.

W Lawrance
November 2014

A Long Long Way

by Sebastian Barry

Synopsis

CHAPTER ONE

The novel opens with the birth of its central character, Willie Dunne, at the end of 1896 in Dublin. We quickly learn that Willie's mother is extremely proud of her son's singing voice, although his father, a senior policeman, would always remain disappointed that Willie's lack of height would make it impossible for his son to join the Dublin Metropolitan Police.

When he reaches the age of 12, Willie's youngest sister, Dolly is born, but their mother dies in childbirth. Due to his inability to follow in his father's footsteps, Willie is apprenticed to a builder named Dempsey - a job which he comes to enjoy. At around this time, Willie first meets Gretta Lawlor, the daughter of a man who had been injured by Willie's father during the 1913 Lockout. Following his injury, Mr Lawlor had joined the army and is now frequently away from home, which enables Willie to spend time alone with Gretta, with whom he has fallen in love.

Willie's simple, happy existence is interrupted by the declaration of the First World War. He decides to enlist, although he finds it difficult to explain exactly why. Gretta does not want him to go and finds his reasons difficult to understand.

CHAPTER TWO

Gretta's confusion begins to make more sense, as it would seem that many men from Ireland have enlisted for contradictory reasons: Southerners because John Redmond had told them that Home Rule would be theirs after the war; Northerners in order to demonstrate their loyalty to England and the Union.

Willie's own enlistment provokes different reactions at home: his father weeps, while his sisters, Maud, Annie and Dolly are excited. He is sent to Fermoy (in County Cork) for training, where he quickly makes friends, but his letter home reveals that he is also homesick.

Once his training is over, Willie embarks for France from his home town. Unfortunately, Dolly could not be persuaded to see her brother leave, so there are no members of his family there to cheer him on his way. He travels towards the war with his new friends, Williams and Clancy, and soon meets the Company Sergeant-Major - a man named Christie Moran. His platoon commander is Captain Pasley. Willie's company are sent into the trenches and quickly discover many of the war's hardships, such as lice, poor food and bombardments.

CHAPTER THREE

Willie and his friends spend some time in the trenches, without seeing any real action. They experience shell-fire, but are not required to do any fighting. The character of Captain Pasley is introduced and immediately causes a stir by looking over the parapet - an action which causes great anxiety to Christie Moran. As one of the side-effects of the continued bombardment, the men discover that no food is being sent up for them, so they go hungry.

The men are sent out at night, into No Man's Land to check and mend the barbed wire along their stretch of the front line. While carrying out this task, they notice a German patrol doing exactly the same opposite them. At first Willie feels afraid, but soon realises that he is with friends now and that, if necessary, he can fight. Once their work is done they all return safely to their trench.

CHAPTER FOUR

Willie has now been away from home for several months, but he is becoming angry that he has still not had a letter from Gretta in all that time. He reminisces about her refusal to marry him, despite their mutual declarations of love. Nonetheless, he writes to her again, telling her of his love and hoping that this might spur her into responding.

The men enjoy a spell in reserve and, during a swim in a nearby river, they learn more about Captain Pasley's background. He talks about his family and their farm and his concerns for his father, who will be having to do all the manual work by himself.

This brief period of respite is short-lived and before long the men are back in the trenches again. During this time, they experience their first gas attack. Initially, they are unsure what to make of this unusual yellow cloud which is approaching over no man's land, but Christie Moran decides they should fall back and gives the order accordingly. Everyone around them also seems to be retreating, but Captain Pasley refuses to leave the trench. Later, Willie finds himself isolated from his comrades. Unsure what to do, he returns to the trench from which he had fled, where he finds the bodies of Williams, Clancy, McNulty and Captain Pasley, and many others.

There are very heavy losses in this gas attack, as a result of which the battalion is taken out of the line and new recruits arrive to replace those killed, or wounded. Captain Sheridan arrives to take the place of Pasley. All these losses and changes make Willie begin to doubt the war: he becomes angry and cannot understand why his new friends had to die.

CHAPTER FIVE

Willie and his friend, Pete O'Hara are on leave in Amiens. One evening, they visit an estaminet and, because he is still angry over Gretta's continued silence, Willie gets drunk and dances with one of the local girls. He and O'Hara are then taken through to a back room where these girls - local prostitutes - ask for money. O'Hara quickly accepts, pays and has sex. Willie is more hesitant but then he too goes ahead. Afterwards, O'Hara seems depressed and the two soldiers leave together.

Willie writes to Gretta telling her of the cold, the boredom and of his love for her, but makes no mention of the incident with the prostitute. A few days later,

O'Hara realises that he has contracted a sexually transmitted disease from the girl with whom he had sex.

Their period of rest comes to an end and Willie and his comrades return to the trenches. Here, one of the new recruits is shot, right next to Willie and lies on the floor of the trench, bleeding and screaming for hours before the stretcher-bearers arrive to take him away. Willie ponders that, if this young man had been a horse, someone would have shot him, rather than leaving him to suffer. A few weeks later, back in billets behind the lines, Willie learns that he will be going home on leave.

CHAPTER SIX

It is now April 1916 and Willie returns home to Dublin Castle on leave. Initially his sister, Maud fails to recognise him, but then he is warmly welcomed. It is decided that Willie should have a bath, so Maud and Annie set about preparing the bathtub. Willie, meanwhile thinks about his father's role in the Lockout. For the first time since it happened, Willie feels disturbed about the deaths of the protestors and by his father's position at that time. His father and Dolly arrive home and both are overjoyed to see Willie. James Dunne bathes his son, as though he were still a child and this action makes Willie feel secure. Once clean and dried, Willie gets dressed into his civilian clothes. During his leave, Willie spends time with Gretta and his family. His final evening is spent with his father, but the next morning, before reporting back to his barracks, Willie finds time to visit Gretta one last time. Again he proposes marriage, but she declines, saying they should wait until the war is over. That night, she visits the barracks and they sneak off into the trees near the gates, where they make love.

CHAPTER SEVEN

The next morning, Willie awakes in the barracks. Desperate for the toilet, he grabs a pot from under the bed and relieves himself. The man in the next bed then accidentally drops his Bible into this pot and, despite Willie retrieving it, the book is ruined. Willie offers the stranger his own Bible, but the man reacts violently to the incident and attempts to strangle Willie. After a short while, however, the man calms down, refuses to accept Willie's Bible and introduces himself as Jesse Kirwan.

Later the troops pass through Dublin, on their way to the ships and
Willie catches a glimpse of Gretta, who has come to see him off. As they
continue their journey, Willie becomes afraid of what he knows awaits them at
the front; he is also worried about the youth and innocence of the new recruits.
At the last minute, however, he calms down and manages to feel almost cheerful.

While the men are waiting on the dockside, preparing to embark, a messenger
arrives and, after some confusion, the men are marched back towards the centre
of Dublin. Here, they witness a cavalry charge up Sackville Street and shots are
fired from the Post Office. A passing civilian offers Willie a pamphlet explaining
what is happening, but Willie declines when his officer threatens to shoot the
civilian. The men are then marched to a different area of the city and ordered to
construct a barricade across the street. Jesse Kirwan, meanwhile, has found one
of the pamphlets and tells Willie that their 'enemy' in this instance is their
fellow Irish-men.

Willie and his comrades come under fire and Willie takes shelter in a doorway,
surrounded by dead soldiers and his wounded Captain. A republican tries to
take Willie as his prisoner, but the Captain shoots him in the neck. Willie goes
to help the wounded man, who tells Willie that he is Irish, not a German, as
Willie had continued to assume. This young man's blood stains Willie's tunic,
but nothing can be done for him and he dies.

Eventually the soldiers board their ship and Willie meets up again with Jesse
Kirwan. Despite Jesse's attempts to explain what has happened, Willie struggles
to make any sense of this recent experience.

CHAPTER EIGHT

Once back in Flanders, Willie and Jesse are sent to separate units. Willie rejoins
his old comrades as they are about to go into the trenches at Hulluch. Willie
tries to explain recent events in Dublin to Christie Moran, who is incensed that
he is fighting on behalf of the men who are causing disorder and chaos at home.
Christie's view is shared by the other men and there seems to be little support
for the rebels. Once back in the trenches, Willie snatches a quiet moment to
write to his father. This letter is full of love and praise for his father's work and
Willie expresses his hopes that his family are well, despite the rebellion.

The next day, the men are warned to expect a gas attack and are reminded that
this time, they must stand firm and not retreat. Father Buckley comes into the

front-line trench to say prayers with the men. When the gas siren is sounded, the men fumble with their new gas masks, but Captain Sheridan removes his in order to give the men a rousing speech. Willie and his comrades are terrified as the gas attack begins and then he notices that a couple of the men have failed to fit their masks properly and are choking and writhing in agony. In his fear, Willie's bowels evacuate and he cries out to his father and grandfather for protection.

After a while, the gas attack is over and the men seem uncertain as to what they should do next. Christie Moran motions for them to prepare for an attack, which swiftly follows. Four Germans enter the trench and Willie attacks one of them with a small axe, wounding him in the face. This man then tears off his gas mask and is overcome by the fumes. Others join in the fight and in the ensuing commotion, Willie is knocked unconscious.

CHAPTER NINE

Willie regains consciousness to find that the German attack has been subdued. He is ordered by Captain Sheridan to run back to Headquarters with a message. Once there, Willie notices how clean everything seems. The officers are very different from the men in the trenches and one of them, Major Stokes, reacts badly to the content of Willie's message, wondering why the Irish troops seem unable to tolerate gas attacks. Another officer, Captain Boston, reminds Stokes that Willie has just come from the front-line and suggests that the Major should calm down. Other messages are also arriving, which show that over three-quarters of those involved in the attack have been either killed or wounded. The major is very insulting towards the Irish in general, and Willie in particular.

Willie returns to the trenches with the message that they must hold out, despite their heavy losses, as no replacements are immediately available. Once back with his friends, Willie joins the burial party and buries the dead German first.

CHAPTER TEN

A few days later, the men are relieved and go back down the line into billets. Here they enjoy a bath, followed by an impromptu concert. In this relaxed atmosphere, Christie Moran thinks about his wife and wishes that he could share his sad secret with the men. His wife had been injured in an accident and Christie knows that he enlisted in the army to escape from here -

not because he does not love her, but because he cannot live with the pity of seeing her every day and remembering how she was before the accident. He fears, however, that the men will laugh at her, so he remains silent on the subject.

CHAPTER ELEVEN

Willie receives a letter from his father, giving details of the events in Dublin and responds to this, clearly shocked by what has happened, but relieved that his family are well. Later, the men read from a newspaper about the executions of the rebel leaders in Dublin. When Willie and Pete O'Hara are alone, they discuss their confusion over these events. They feel that they must be the enemies of the rebels and yet, these are also their countrymen. They also agree that the executions were wrong.

Willie continues writing his letter to his father, in which he declares his wish that the rebels had not been shot and telling of his own experience in the doorway in Dublin. He says that he also feels proud to be serving his country. This letter appears to show Willie's continued confusion about events in Ireland and he seems to be seeking reassurance and guidance from his father. He also sends a postcard to Gretta, in response to one he had received from her, showing the ruins of Sackville Street in Dublin.

CHAPTER TWELVE

News continues to come in from Ireland and the men still fear for their families. There is a great deal of confusion and division of opinions about the rebellion, made worse by the fact that the men feel removed from it and therefore cannot have any influence over events. In addition, they are confused about the war and its lack of meaning or progress.

Father Buckley visits Willie in the billet and tells him that Jesse Kirwan is facing a court martial and has asked to see Willie. Jesse, it would seem, has already been tried and punished for disobedience and is now refusing to obey any orders at all. In addition, he is refusing to talk to anyone, or eat any food. Willie is surprised by Jesse's request to see him, as their friendship was so fleeting and is initially reluctant to agree. Already tired of the war himself, Willie feels that meeting Jesse again in these circumstances will only bring him more doubt and despair. Eventually, however, he agrees.

The Battle of the Somme begins and, although not yet involved themselves, Willie and his friends hear news of the men from Ulster who took part, at great cost. On 3rd July, Willie accompanies Father Buckley to visit Jesse Kirwan, who is being held in a working abattoir. While Father Buckley briefly speaks to Jesse, Willie talks to the corporal on guard and discovers that Major Stokes is due to be the chairman of the court martial. When they meet, Jesse tells Willie that he is refusing to fight because the Ireland which he came out to defend and protect does not exist any more; the shooting of the rebel leaders means that Ireland will be more divided than ever and he can see no point in returning to that. He wants the army to save him the trouble and shoot him. Willie is confused by Jesse's statements, but tries to persuade him to change his mind. Once he sees that Jesse cannot be dissuaded from his chosen course, Willie gives him his Bible and the men part.

CHAPTER THIRTEEN

A few weeks later, in August, Jesse Kirwan is executed by firing squad. At his funeral, Father Buckley tells Willie about Jesse's family background: a sad tale which haunts Willie. Later, struggling to understand what has happened, Willie speaks to Pete O'Hara. Neither of them is really able to comprehend the justification in shooting a 'volunteer', just because he no longer wishes to 'help'.

O'Hara, a regular soldier, tells Willie a story, from the early days of the war, about a Belgian woman that he and his company had discovered. She had been tied up, raped and mutilated. They had released her, although unsure whether her ill-treatment was the result of her own collaboration with the Germans or whether her injuries had been inflicted by the enemy. While helping this woman, they had come under attack and some of the men had been killed, while the remainder sheltered in a ditch. Once the attack was over, one of the surviving men had raped the woman and O'Hara had held her down during the assault. Willie is overcome with anger and strikes O'Hara viciously. The two men argue, as O'Hara tries to justify his actions, claiming that Willie would have done the same thing in his place. Willie is unsure: he wonders whether they have all lost control; whether civilisation even exists any more.

CHAPTER FOURTEEN

Willie's company is sent back into the trenches, in the hope that they can capitalise on advances made at Guillemont and push on further. Firstly the men must cross the old no man's land, which is littered with the dismembered bodies of their fellow soldiers. They briefly occupy the German trenches - now the British front line - before being order to go over the top.

The men attack in the direction of Guinchy [sic] and come under machine-gun fire. Captain Sheridan is shot, but the men carry on until they reach their target. Here they fight hand-to-hand with the Germans until they surrender. Willie and his surviving comrades return to their original starting trench, where they are hailed as heroes. However, they discover that Captain Sheridan is dead and they feel anything but heroic.

CHAPTER FIFTEEN

Willie receives an unexpected letter from his sister, Maud, saying that their father is angry with Willie over his attitude towards the rebellion. Willie, however, remains unsure as to what can have caused such offence. There is a regimental boxing match between a man from Ulster and another from the south. Other entertainments follow and Willie notices how many new faces there are. His friend, Joe Kielty, tells Willie that he enlisted because a girl had given him a white feather.

Later, when Willie goes to bed, he unexpectedly begins to weep. He feels depressed about the war which he begins to believe, will never end.

CHAPTER SIXTEEN

The men go back into the trenches, their numbers having been bolstered by new recruits. The new arrivals are, however, not Irish, but English. One of them, Timmy Weekes from London, introduces the others to literature. There is also a new commanding officer, named Biggs. They pass a bitterly cold winter.

Willie writes to his family and Gretta, but hears nothing back from either her or his father. He attends confession and asks forgiveness for having had sex with the prostitute in Amiens. Father Buckley tells him not to worry about this and they move on to discuss Willie's feelings about his family. Father Buckley tries to reassure Willie that it is alright for him to think for himself, but Willie remains unsure.

CHAPTER SEVENTEEN

The men go up into the front line for the Battle of Messines and while they are waiting to go over the top, Christie Moran finally tells them about his wife's deformity. It would seem that she had accidentally set light to the bed and burned her hand. He reveals that he enlisted because she could no longer work and they needed the money. The reaction of his men surprises him: rather than the anticipated laughter, he receives their understanding and sympathy.

At the allotted time, mines are detonated and then the men go over the top. They push forwards to the ridge where Christie Moran single-handedly takes a machine-gun post. The men reach their objective and occupy a German trench. Biggs soon realises that Christie Moran, Joe Kielty and a few others have gone on too far ahead, so he leaves Willie in charge and goes off to find them. After an hour, Moran and the others return, but Biggs has been killed. Despite this, progress has been so good, that they wonder whether this might have been the last great battle of the war.

A few weeks later, still feeling elated after their victory, Christie is awarded a medal for his bravery. Willie goes on a bayonetting course and, in his absence, they are visited by the King. Willie is disappointed that he missed the King's visit, but gets a good account of it from Christie Moran, who is impressed, despite all he had previously said against the monarchy. The men are then moved again - this time to Ypres.

CHAPTER EIGHTEEN

The men hear the news that Willie Redmond - brother of John - has been killed. They are all upset, but particularly Father Buckley, who had often praised Willie Redmond. In August, the weather changes and it rains heavily. The bombardment continues and the men go up to the front line. Willie, Joe Kielty and Timmy Weekes discuss the futility of the war.

They spend two days in appalling trenches prior to going over the top. Crossing no man's land, they come under fierce enemy fire, but Willie, Joe, Christie and Timmy Weekes manage to reach their objective. Initially, their new commanding officer fails to appear, but then comes up with the second wave. Willie and his comrades are then relieved and fall back to their starting trench. Here Willie learns that Father Buckley has been killed, while helping at an Aid Post. This saddens and surprises Willie who believes he had seen the Padre tending to the wounded in no man's land. It would seem, however that Father Buckley never left the Aid Post at all.

After weeks in the trenches, Christie tells Willie that he's been granted home leave - a request evidently made by Father Buckley before he died. As he is about to leave, Christie gives Willie his medal for luck.

CHAPTER NINETEEN

Willie returns to Dublin. Dolly is the first to greet him and is overjoyed. Maud and Annie are equally pleased but their father is merely cordial at first. Then he berates Willie for sympathising with the rebels, which he takes as a personal betrayal against himself, the family, his position and his beliefs. He refuses to listen to Willie's explanations and feeling hurt, Willie leaves.

In the face of this disappointment, Willie's thoughts turn immediately to Gretta. He finds her in her lodgings, feeding a young baby, which she says belongs to herself and her husband. She tells Willie that she received a letter from one of his friends which changed everything in their relationship. Willie reads the letter, which reveals that he had sex with the prostitute in Amiens. He is devastated to have lost Gretta and now feels unworthy of her. With nowhere else to go, he winds up at a hostel for the night.

CHAPTER TWENTY

While still on leave, Willie goes to visit Captain Pasley's family. He passes through Dublin, where some boys throw a piece of granite and spit at him. They assume that he is English because he is in uniform. Willie feels numbed by events surrounding his father and Gretta wondering whether he was a fool to have gone to the war.

When he nears Pasley's home, Willie has to ask directions of a rector. This man shows Willie more kindness and consideration than anyone else during his leave. Once he finds the Captain's house, Willie is warmly welcomed by Pasley's mother, who is touched by his thoughtfulness. Willie realises how much he misses the Captain and all of his other dead friends. When Pasley's father returns from work, he is also pleased to see Willie, who finds himself repeating phrases used by the Captain.

When the time comes for Willie to depart from Dublin, Maud, Annie and Dolly go to the station, but only Dolly goes onto the platform: the other two remain behind the barrier.

CHAPTER TWENTY-ONE

Back at the front, Willie turns 21, but receives no acknowledgement of this milestone from his family. He is in a quiet sector of the front and here, he and his friends pass Christmas and New Year. Willie wonders who could have sent the letter to Gretta and discusses it with O'Hara, who agrees that to write something like that was the worst thing one soldier could do to another.

As the weeks pass, everyone seems more anxious than usual - as though they are anticipating an attack. Eventually the Germans launch an offensive and initially Willie and his comrades stand their ground. Christie Moran, however, decides that they should pull back, which they do, leaving Joe Kielty to cover their retreat. The men enter a wood, but find that the Germans are already there. They manage to defend themselves and re-group. Pete O'Hara is wounded and just before he dies, he confesses to Willie that it was he who sent the letter to Gretta in revenge for Willie's reaction to the story about the Belgian girl. Willie is angry, but Pete is contrite and dies before he can fully explain his actions.

The next morning, the bombardment begins again and Willie is hit by a shell. He seems unsure as to where he is and starts to hallucinate before losing consciousness.

CHAPTER TWENTY-TWO

Willie is now in hospital and slowly recovering from his injuries. He also seems to be suffering from shell-shock, as his head and left arm shake uncontrollably. He receives a letter from Christie Moran, showing that the sergeant-major must have carried Willie back to a Casualty Clearing Station behind the lines. The letter also tells him that Timmy Weekes is dead.

An officer visits Willie and tells him that his battalion has been almost wiped out and that there is a near revolution in Ireland. It would seem that many believe there will now never be Home Rule in Ireland. During this visit, Willie struggles to control his limbs and his speech, to such an extent, that the officer leaves - unable to communicate properly.

As Willie's wounds heal, he discovers that the markings of Christie Moran's medal, which had been in his breast pocket, have been branded onto his chest by the heat of the blast.

One day, he asks the nurse if she will give him a cuddle. Despite her initial hesitation, she eventually agrees and cradles him like a child. Miraculously, he stops shaking. As his health returns, Willie writes to his father, explaining his shell-shock and saying that, despite their differences, he has the greatest love and admiration for his father.

Willie feels as though death now controls everything and that man has no say in his own future. He also loses his faith - not only in God, but in everything which he has always held sacred.

CHAPTER TWENTY-THREE

Willie returns to France. His regiment contains very few Irishmen, partly because they are no longer enlisting and also because the establishment view appears to be that the Irish cannot be trusted to fight anyway. There seems to be a general state of confusion: the Irish civilian population are now critical of the men who are fighting for the British while the senior army are accusing these same men of cowardice.

Willie is surprised to find that he is actually looking forward to going back to the front. He knows what to expect and, although he is afraid, it is the only place where he now feels as though he belongs. When he arrives, he discovers that Joe Kielty and Christie Moran are the only friends who are left. He learns that Joe, who had stayed behind to cover their withdrawal from the trench, was able to survive because the German shells fell short of their target, killing their own men.

In the summer of 1918, Major Stokes is found hanged, having committed suicide. The American troops arrive and the Allies are making strong advances. As they pass through Belgium, following the retreating German troops, Willie is struck by the devastation of the country. He begins to reflect on returning to Ireland, which has now changed forever and he begins to understand Jesse Kirwan's point of view. He feels that the cause for which he was fighting has died. He questions everything: his beliefs, his country, his loyalties, his future.

The Germans make one last stand and, while in the trenches opposite, Willie hears one of them singing 'Silent Night', which leads him to reflect upon his own loneliness and the fact that he has no-one and nowhere to which he can return. Willie sings back to the German and is shot by a sniper. Joe Kielty catches his falling body, but Willie dies.

After his death, a letter arrives from Willie's father in which he apologises for his behaviour and asks for Willie's forgiveness. This letter, together with the remainder of his belongings, are returned to his family. Christie and Joe bury his body and mark the grave.

CHARACTER ANALYSIS

In this section, we have provided firstly a summary of the traits of each character and how these are demonstrated by their actions throughout the story. Secondly, we have offered a critical analysis of the portrayal of these characters and how this affects the novel as a whole. In addition, the next chapter, Critical Comparisons, features a section on how other authors have dealt with the creation and development of their characters.

1. WILLIE DUNNE

Born in December 1896, William Dunne is the only son of James Dunne, a senior Irish policeman. His memories of childhood are, generally, warm and happy, despite his mother's death when he was twelve years old. He seems to have passed a secure and contented youth, under the watchful eye of his father. His relationship with his father is, not untypically for the time and class, based upon Willie's respect and continued acknowledgement that the older man's views are always correct. As Willie advances into adulthood, both of them long for him to become sufficiently tall to join the police force. Unfortunately, this is not to be and they are both bitterly disappointed. Despite this, Willie finds that his apprenticeship to Dempsey, the builder, provides him with an enjoyable occupation about which he feels enthusiastic.

To add to his happiness, Willie meets Gretta Lawlor. However, as the daughter of a man who had been involved in the 1913 Lockout, Willie decides it would be prudent to keep his romance a secret from his father. He and Gretta seem well suited and Willie quickly realises that he is in love. The beginning of the First World War interrupts this contented scene and he decides almost immediately that he will enlist. He does this partly to defend Gretta - and by extension, his country - but also to please his father and make up for his disappointment at Willie being unable to become a policeman. Gretta cannot really understand Willie's decision, but he goes anyway. Prior to departing, he proposes marriage, presumably to demonstrate his love and commitment, but she declines. Her refusal does not diminish his affection for her.

Willie's attachment to his home, as well as his youth, is demonstrated in his first letter home which he sends from the training camp. He reminisces about his home life, recalling evenings spent with his father and sisters. This letter also shows that Willie makes friends easily, exhibiting a pleasant nature.

As Willie spends more time away from home, he becomes more thoughtful. He tries to empathise with the French people, for example, wondering how he would feel if the war were being fought on Irish soil.

His first contact with danger, when he and his comrades go over the top one night to mend the barbed wire, shows us the youthful innocence of Willie mixed with his new-found courage and trust in his fellow-soldiers. His initial fear melts away as he realises that he is capable of fighting, Willie's first experience of death, however, has a much more profound effect on him. Many of his new friends are killed in the first gas attack at St Julian [sic], but the death which haunts him most is that of Captain Pasley. Pasley's family is known to Willie's father, but the officer had also managed to command Willie's respect by his words and actions, so Willie feels his death greatly.

By now, a few doubts are beginning to grow in Willie's mind. He cannot understand why his friends and the Captain died - no purpose was served and nothing was gained. Also, he has heard nothing from Gretta since they parted in Dublin, many months earlier. He has written to her often and he knows that she can write, so assumes that she chooses not to respond. His frustration, together with his drunkenness, is what leads to the episode with the prostitute in Amiens. Afterwards, Willie seems to feel guilty, so he writes to Gretta expressing his love for her as though he hopes that by doing this he can expunge his offence.

His war-weariness starts to show when a young recruit is shot, Willie is initially reluctant to offer any help. Even when he does move nearer to the young man, he cannot assist and this makes him feel impotent, which merely adds to his fatigue. It is, perhaps, fortunate that Willie is granted a spell of leave at this time. This first visit home enables him to return to scenes of happiness when the war seems like a distant memory. Unfortunately, this visit ends badly when Willie is called upon to fight the rebels in the streets of Dublin. This episode marks and onset of confusion, as well as a rude awakening to the reality of civil war. Willie, along with most of his comrades, struggles to come to terms with events in Dublin and to equate them with his experiences at the front.

At about this time, Willie first meets Jesse Kirwan. Their's is a hesitant, slightly withdrawn friendship, which is hardly surprising being as they come from very different backgrounds. Willie seems unsure about Jesse and this adds to his confused state of mind.

The second gas attack terrifies Willie, especially as he has already witnessed the consequences of this terrible weapon. This fear, coupled with his building adrenalin lead to his being able to strike out at the attacking German soldier with surprising ferocity. It is interesting to note that when cornered by the young Irish rebel in the Dublin doorway, Willie has hesitated to draw his rifle. In the trenches, however, his survival instinct has come to the fore. This death will also haunt Willie and the German soldier later appears in Willie's dreams.

Willie, we are told, is now beginning to mature. When confronted and verbally abused by Major Stokes, Willie takes the sensible option: he does not retaliate, but equally, he holds his ground and refuses to just accept the Major's insults. This shows that Willie is developing an independent streak, which is also reflected in his letter to his father. Here, he demonstrates his belief that his age and experiences should entitle him to voice an opinion, even though this may not reflect the view of his father. In spite of his growing maturity, however, Willie still looks to his father for guidance. When this is not forthcoming, this adds to Willie's confusion and he feels that, if he is old enough to fight and die for his country, he should most certainly be allowed to voice his opinion about it.

Willie's war-weariness comes to the fore again when he is asked to speak to Jesse Kirwan. He feels that such a conversation can only drag him further down and is reluctant to help. By appealing to Willie's conscience, Father Buckley gets him to agree to the meeting. Willie's supposition proves accurate as this meeting and Jesse's execution, we are told, have a great impact on the young soldier, and he realises that he will never be the same again.

Pete O'Hara's sordid tale of the treatment of a young Belgian girl provokes a violent reaction from Willie, who lashes out at his friend. This response demonstrates Willie's fear that they are becoming inured to the barbaric elements of war and that they may be permanently lost to civilisation. He strikes out, rather than face his own demons. Willie's second visit home proves to be devastating. His father's mockery and Gretta's rejection of him push Willie to the point of despair and he is only saved by his visit to the home of Captain Pasley. Here he receives a warm welcome, but is also reminded of how much he misses his dead comrades.

Willie's resignation to his fate seems to be sealed after his injury. At this point, he sees only a bleak future, entirely controlled by death and war. As such, he looks forward to returning to the front and his comrades: they have become his reality and no matter how hopeless his future might seem, he feels more comfortable with his friends than anywhere else.

CRITICAL ANALYSIS OF WILLIE DUNNE'S CHARACTER

As the central character in this novel, Willie Dunne is crucial to the plot: the reader must be able to relate to his character in order to maintain interest and unify the whole, rather than it being a series of events, loosely joined together. In this respect, Willie Dunne is disappointing. He does not seem like a plausible character, not aided by the scant introduction to him. His first seventeen years are covered in ten pages, so the reader has little idea about his childhood, opinions, background or hopes for the future, as these are all glossed over and dismissed, in order to move swiftly into the war scenes. The problem with this is that, as Willie hurtles towards the front line, he still feels like a stranger, thus making it difficult for the reader to relate to him and his reactions.

These inadequacies in 'fleshing-out' Willie's character continue to occur throughout the book. For example, his relationship with Gretta is so briefly described that it can hardly be taken seriously. There is no satisfactory explanation for her lack of correspondence. We are told that she is tired at the end of the day, but this is a barely sufficient reason for never writing a word in more than 12 months between Willie going to France and his first spell of leave. Later, even when she does write, she merely sends a postcard. This leads the reader to doubt the strength of their relationship, which supposedly means so much to Willie that, when he loses her, he thinks he might die. This powerful intensity of emotion has, however, never truly been demonstrated between them - we are simply told that it exists.

The reader is continually being told that Willie has 'changed' and, while there is evidence of a slightly growing maturity, he never really exhibits these alterations in his character. We are informed, for example, that Willie feels the war has changed him, that seeing his friends die has affected him so greatly that he can make so sense of it all and yet he continues to behave in exactly the same way at the end of the book, as at the beginning.

Another problem with this central character is the sheer quantity of catastrophes which befall him. His beloved and respected father mocks and rejects him, only apologising when it is too late; his girlfriend immediately believes a letter written about him and marries another man; Willie is involved in almost every major battle on the Western Front, plus the Irish rebellion; most of his friends are killed; he is wounded, shell-shocked and finally dies, singing a Christmas carol at the beginning of October, a few weeks prior to the Armistice. The reader can easily adopt an attitude of waiting for the next incident to befall him and wondering just how much Willie's character can tolerate. Yet, fundamentally, he remains exactly the same person at the end of the story as he was at the beginning. None of these life-changing events really cause a great reaction or alteration to his essential personality.

We are also told that Willie has become war-weary and embittered, confused by both the war at home and that in which he is participating, but there is no really substantial evidence of this. Willie has fleeting conversations with some of his comrades about the futility of the war but these are so contrived that they feel unnatural and forced upon the characters - because the author presumably believes that they should be feeling this way. These are not thoughts or emotions which seem to have come naturally, or to have been developed through Willie's experiences and thoughts.

Willie's character is not assisted in its plausibility by the fact that some of the events which happen to him are almost too artificial to be believed or taken seriously. Two such examples occur in quick succession, following his injury. The nurse discovers that an imprint of Christie Moran's medal has been branded onto Willie's chest - over his heart, thus clumsily implying that his heart will always belong to Ireland. Secondly, and more importantly, Willie's shell-shock, suddenly manifested in an uncontrollable shaking, is 'miraculously' cured by the nurse holding him and cradling him like a young child. The first of these episodes feels contrived, the second is almost too ludicrous to be believed. More serious than the reader's interpretation of these events, however, is the author's implication that a man, who has been driven, by his hideous experiences to the point of losing physical, mental and emotional control, can be cured simply by a cuddle from a pretty young nurse. This is nothing short of insulting to those men who suffered and endured the numerous treatments for this condition, many of which failed to bring a satisfactory response. This episode not only discredits the intelligence of the reader, it maligns those who suffered the torture and indignity that was shell-shock.

2. GRETTA LAWLOR

Gretta Lawlor is the young girl with whom Willie Dunne falls in love during the year prior to the First World War. The couple meet as the result of differences between their respective fathers and it is these differences which go on to shape their relationship. Gretta's father had been involved in the Lockout in Dublin, which started in August 1913. During the conflict, the police, including Willie's father had baton-charged the strikers, resulting in many injuries, amongst which was Gretta's father. Feeling guilty, James Dunne had been taking gifts of food to Mr Lawlor but, sensing that his presence was unwelcome, Mr Dunne asks Willie to go on his behalf.

Willie's attraction to Gretta is immediate and physical. At the time of their initial meeting, he is sixteen and she is three years younger. Before long, they are thrown together on a more regular basis, as Gretta's father, having lost his job, decides to join the army, leaving his daughter alone. Willie visits her regularly, to make sure that she is alright, but also because he enjoys spending time with her. Although he has fallen n love with Gretta, Willie chooses to keep her a secret from his family, knowing that none of them would approve of his choice.

When war is declared, Gretta does not understand why Willie feels the need to enlist, other than for his own desire to please his father - a sentiment of which she can approve. She feels no loyalty to the British and knows that her own father had only joined up for the money. So, Willie's other reasons for fighting make no sense to Gretta. She abides by her father's wishes and knows that he would never undertake such an action.

Just before departing, Willie proposes marriage to Gretta, but she refuses. She also neglects to write to him during his absence. When he returns on leave and questions her about this, she claims tiredness as her excuse. Similarly, although she says that she loves him, there is always the underlying sense that she is holding back.Gretta rejects Willie's second marriage proposal, this time citing the war as her reason. It would seem that Gretta may have a greater understanding than Willie of the potential problems which might arise from a union between these two characters. Their different backgrounds, beliefs and aspirations cause an amount of hesitancy in Gretta, probably enhanced by the fact that she also needs security and is probably looking for someone more like herself.

It is interesting to note that when Gretta does eventually write to Willie, she does not send a letter, such as the other men receive, but a postcard of the devastated Sackville Street. This image may be Gretta's way of reminding Willie where she believes his responsibilities lie - namely at home, rather than fighting for the British on foreign soil. Equally, she may simply want to show him the damage done by British artillery to Irish homes and property, again to make him question his loyalties.

Gretta's reaction to the letter from Pete O'Hara is to immediately believe its contents. She writes to Willie (although he does not receive this letter) to tell him that she cannot go on as before and that everything between them has changed. Almost immediately, Gretta marries another man and bears him a child, which shows her underlying need for security, but also, perhaps that her feelings for Willie were not that strong in the first place. When Willie first sees Gretta nursing her baby, he immediately knows that the child cannot be his, but he remains concerned for her and continues to believe the best. Gretta, on the other hand, is not so generous towards Willie, having automatically believed the letter and assumed the worst of him. The man whom Gretta has chosen to marry is from her own class and works with her father, and presumably shares her opinion about the soldiers who have gone to fight for the British - of whom both Gretta and her father seem to disapprove. This may be another demonstration of her doubts about the long-term differences between herself and Willie. In addition, her husband, not be a soldier, provides her with the security of knowing that he will not be going off to war or to his death. She does not mention that she loves her husband - only that he is a good man - but perhaps the certainty and security with which he provides her is of greater importance than the passion and uncertainty of life with Willie.

CRITICAL ANALYSIS OF GRETTA LAWLOR'S CHARACTER

The main criticism of the portrayal of Gretta Lawlor is that she is too flimsy. We are not given sufficient information about her past, her upbringing or her personality and she, therefore, feels like a 'token' female, inserted into the plot simply as a device. Even then, however, she falls short of expectations as she fails to fulfil any tangible role. One could argue that she represents home and reminds us of how much the young soldiers have to lose. Yet her relationship with Willie is so one-sided and insubstantial that she fails to achieve even this minor 'home-front' representation. Alternatively, she may be meant to demonstrate the divide between those in the working class slums and the slightly better off; those in favour of the rebellion and those against. This clumsy representation of the divisions of class, upbringing and beliefs also fails, mainly because Gretta's extreme youth makes it difficult for the reader to assess her judgements, especially as they are mainly echoes of her father's words, rather than her own thoughts, gained through her experiences.

The only other role with which Gretta could be credited is that she serves to enhance the reader's sympathy for Willie. She is portrayed as relatively cold and remorseless, while Willie is the more thoughtful and generous. As he undergoes all sorts of hideous events, she cannot even be bothered to write to him. Therefore, when she receives Pete O'Hara's letter and marries another man, the reader feels that it is Willie who has been betrayed, by both of them, and Gretta becomes yet another in the long list of catastrophes which befall the leading character.

Even as a straightforward literary romantic interest, Gretta falls short. Once again, her extreme youth is a problem here, but also their 'romance' is so scantily described that it fails to hold the reader's interest, coming across as more of a teenage crush, than an intense and passionate affair, the memory of which will sustain Willie throughout his time in France - which we are told is the case.

Like Willie, Gretta seems to be an unrealistic character, whose supposed significance in Willie's life lacks any explanation or credence. Without this, it is impossible to take her or their relationship seriously. It is not enough to simply be told that one character feels a particular emotion: their actions must also confirm this.

3. JAMES DUNNE

James Dunne, Willie's father, plays a significant role in the novel, in that he demonstrates the 'establishment' viewpoint of the war, and the Irish Rebellion. He also reminds the reader of Willie's childhood and upbringing and that, initially, Willie's opinions and actions are based around loyalty to his father.

James Dunne's life, although professionally successful, has been marred by tragedy. The death of his wife has left him to raise their four children alone and he seems to have managed this well. In addition, while bringing up his children, he has also managed to gain promotion within the police force, which shows him to be a determined and ambitious man - one might almost say, single-minded. He is also a man who, true to the time and his position in society, is used to getting his own way and expects others to fall in with his way of thinking. So his older daughters keep the house and are expected to obey his every word without question, while Willie and he go out to work. His children seem to be told what they should think, rather than being encouraged to form their own opinions. This contrasts well with Mr Lawlor, who always expects others to know their own minds.

Mr Lawlor and James Dunne only come into contact as they have been on opposing sides during the Lockout of Autumn 1913. His guilt at having injured Mr Lawlor shows a more sensitive and fair side to James Dunne's character. He had chosen not to wear his uniform to visit Mr Lawlor, to save any embarrassment and Lawlor had still rejected his offerings. This episode, however, shows a certain naivety and stubbornness on the part of James Dunne. There are clear differences between himself and Mr Lawlor, especially regarding their politics. It is, therefore, highly unlikely that the two men would ever have seen eye-to-eye. Mr Lawlor does not seek James Dunne's good wishes because the policeman's behaviour had been just as he would have expected. James Dunne, on the other hand, seems to seek Mr Lawlor's forgiveness - little understanding that the growing differences between them are unlikely to ever be bridged.

James Dunne takes his own role and position in society very seriously, as he does his own opinions. Although he believes that he should have a considerable influence over others, he also fails to account for the effects of that influence. So, throughout Willie's young life, he has stressed the importance of his son becoming tall enough to become a policeman. Willie's failure to achieve a sufficient height causes them both an amount of disappointment. However, this is more keenly felt by Willie, who is helpless to change the situation but is constantly reminded of his own perceived 'failure'. In addition, when war is declared, James Dunne speaks vehemently about a man's duty to fight for the King - seeming not to realise that his young son would promptly go and enlist.

James Dunne's rejection of his son is cruel. He laughs at Willie, mocking his opinions because they do not tally with his own. He seems to feel that by questioning the justification of the rebellion, Willie has betrayed him personally and he completely fails to understand Willie's confusion over the situation in which he and his friends have found themselves. James Dunne insults Willie, portraying his own suffering as worse and more important than that of Willie and his comrades. Although James Dunne eventually sees reason and writes a letter of apology to his Willie, this only arrives after his son's death, so neither man would ever know or understand the other's motives. James had left it to Willie to make the first move and had only written in response to an appeasing letter from his son. His stubborn self-importance therefore prevents him from repairing the damage and pain his earlier words had caused.

CRITICAL ANALYSIS OF JAMES DUNNE'S CHARACTER

James Dunne is initially portrayed as a straightforward, loyal, decent, family man, who like many in his position, commands respect from those around him. We are also shown that he is a reasonable, fair-minded man and hence he tries to help Mr Lawlor to make amends for having injured him. However, this impression soon begins to fall apart. Whilst it is perfectly conceivable and realistic that a man in his position at that time would have been over-bearing and domineering, it seems almost incomprehensible that a man of reasonable intelligence, who has clearly cared deeply for his only son and wept when he went away to the war, could treat him with such disdain. Here we have a character who proclaims the importance of family values and yet he makes absolutely no attempt to understand his son's situation. This portrayal feels manufactured, as, based on his previous behaviour, the reader might expect James Dunne to sit his son down, listen to his viewpoint and then try to explain his perception of the situation and rationally bring Willie round to his way of thinking. His mockery and rejection of Willie seems out of character and yet it is much more dramatic and enhances the sense that Willie has no-one left at home to really care about what happens to him.

Sebastian Barry's use of James Dunne's character is two-fold. Firstly he is there to provide yet another calamity in the life of Willie Dunne. Secondly, he demonstrates the deep divisions which Home Rule and the rebellion caused in Ireland. However, even this fails to work properly as James Dunne's opinions are too obvious, while his son's change of heart is never fully realised or explained and only amounts to an element of doubt and confusion, rather than any real commitment to either stance.

4. MINOR CHARACTERS

CHRISTIE MORAN

In the absence of his own father, once he leaves home, Christie Moran becomes a father-figure for Willie Dunne. He influences Willie's thoughts in a way which James Dunne had previously, so, for example, Christie's anger about the rebels and the rebellion cause Willie to doubt his own views and he begins to question what is right and wrong. This role is thrust upon Christie Moran, as the Company Sergeant-Major, which means he is in charge of the men and they, naturally, look up to him. In addition, he earns their respect by his actions: not only is he brave, but he seems to instinctively know what to do - even when others are doubtful, he makes clear decisions and acts accordingly.

Moran has had an unhappy past, the injury to his wife seems to have placed a barrier between them and he has enlisted to escape the sadness of seeing her. He clearly loves his wife and they write often. Initially, he is reluctant to speak about her to the men, partly for fear that they will mock, and partly because he is unwilling to discuss his private life with the 'ranks'. This does not mean that he feels he is superior to them, but he understands the need to maintain discipline. When he does eventually reveal the truth about his wife, Moran seems genuinely surprised and affected by their sympathetic reaction.

When awarded a medal for his bravery, Moran makes light of this and gives the medal to Willie to bring him luck. He regards his own actions as quite normal and not at all noteworthy. This can also be seen when he recalls carrying Willie from the battlefield to a casualty clearing station. Again Moran plays down his own role in saving Willie's life.

The reader senses that Christie Moran is actually quite fond of his men. He seems to accept their deaths, when they come, as an inevitable part of war and, yet he makes a point of commending Willie for visiting Captain Pasley's family. He is also concerned to note the exact spot where he and Joe Kielty bury Willie, so that he will be able to have a named grave.

These small actions demonstrate Moran's comradeship and compassion, which he continually attempts to disguise.

PETE O'HARA

As friends, Pete O'Hara and Willie Dunne share many experiences, although O'Hara is a more practised soldier, being as he served in the regular army in India before the First World War. One of their shared experiences is their visit to the prostitutes in Amiens. This event leads directly to O'Hara's main role in the novel - namely that he writes to Gretta, revealing Willie's infidelity - although making no mention of his own indiscretion. The letter causes Gretta to abandon any idea of a future with Willie, which in turn leads to Willie's greatest unhappiness. Although O'Hara knows that he has been directly responsible for this turn of events, he continues to behave like a friend to Willie, denouncing the man who sent the letter and seemingly incredulous that one soldier could do such a thing to one of his comrades.

The story which O'Hara tells about the rape and eventual death of the young Belgian girl shows a clear division between the two men. Willie is appalled by this story and cannot understand why O'Hara tells it. He reacts violently and a rift occurs between the friends which never really heals. Even on his deathbed, as he lies in Willie's arms, O'Hara cannot explain his own reactions. He confesses to sending the letter and says he regrets it and yet his explanation of feeling humiliated seems unsatisfactory.

JESSE KIRWAN

Jesse's role within the novel is very minor. His initial meeting with Willie is both strange and brief. He reacts angrily to his Bible dropping into a pot of Willie's urine, by trying to strangle him. Then, however, he suddenly and inexplicably calms down and introduces himself. Jesse is a 'volunteer' in every sense - a supporter of Home Rule, who has followed the edicts of John Redmond and taken up arms to further their cause. However, others who also want Home Rule have chosen to continue to fight for independence at home and this makes the rebellion in which he and Willie become entangled, a difficult situation for Jesse.

Initially, that is the limit of his association with Willie. However, when the two men meet again, the circumstances are just as strange as those of their first meeting. Jesse has been arrested for refusing to obey orders and has asked to see Willie. Despite their brief acquaintance he wants to unburden his worries to someone and believes that Willie alone will understand his state of mind. He explains that he wants the army to shoot him because his homeland and everything for which he was fighting has disappeared. He does not believe there will ever be Home Rule in Ireland and if the Irish can fight against each other then he can see no hope for the future. Although he could go back to the trenches and die there - like so many others - he wants his death to have more significance and be of greater inconvenience to the British Army than to merely become another casualty of the war. Perhaps he also feels the need for some solidarity with the rebels in Ireland, who have come under attack from the British army and wishes his death to be at their hands too.

This episode shows that for an Irishman fighting in the First World War, it was not merely his experiences in that conflict which would affect him, but also the events which were unfolding at home. The confusion caused by the rebellion and its consequences force Jesse to re-examine his role in the conflict and, in his own way, he rebels against the establishment.

CRITICAL ANALYSIS OF MINOR CHARACTERS

Many of the minor characters in the novel feel clichéd. For example, Jesse Kirwan is a 'volunteer' in every sense of the word, who loses so much faith in the causes for which he had been fighting, that he actively seeks his own death at the hands of the British. His introduction into the plot feels false and contrived, being as his initial reaction to Willie is so extreme. This is made worse by the fact that he then calms down so abruptly and almost immediately becomes Willie's friends. His subsequent behaviour also serves to give Willie another problem, to add to his catalogue of woes. Jesse chooses to unburden himself upon the hapless Willie, who must then carry the knowledge of Jesse's death and his past with him. The imprisonment of Jesse in a working abbatoir does nothing to help in the realism of his character, as it seems to have been done merely to provide Sebastian Barry with the opportunity to compare the death of a bullock with the slaughter of the men. This scene is also uncannily reminiscent of Wilfred Owen's *Anthem for Doomed Youth* - even to the point where the animal is described as 'praying'.

The death of Jesse Kirwan allows Barry to introduce another controversial aspect of the war: the executions of serving men. He compares the execution of Kirwan - and by extension, others like him - with those of the rebel leaders in Ireland, forcing the reader to question the validity of such punishments. While it could be argued that there were many many unjust executions during the conflict, it is too simple to look back with 21st century eyes and imply that they were all wrong.

Pete O'Hara's role is simply to demonstrate the depths to which a man may fall, once he has become sufficiently war-weary. O'Hara - as a regular soldier before the war - demonstrates that the normal rules of friendship and decency have ceased to apply and that self-preservation becomes of paramount importance. Like Jesse, Pete's reactions to various events are often inexplicable. For example, he seems disenchanted following his visit to the prostitutes in Amiens. This may be because it reminds him of the episode with the Belgian girl, or because he feels ashamed of his own behaviour. However, his character is so sketchily portrayed that the reader is left to draw his own conclusions as to his motives.

Of all the minor characters, Christie Moran feels the most genuine and realistic. He is perhaps not so stereotypical, but a self-effacing, soldier who earns the respect of his men by his actions. Barry occasionally uses Moran's character to demonstrate that the ordinary soldiers sometimes had more sense than their superiors - to enhance the 'lions led by donkeys' theme. In addition, as Willie's father-figure, Moran's character provides a contrast with that of Willie's own father. Despite his hardships, Moran is philosophical and stoic, while James Dunne refuses to see Willie's perspective and cruelly rejects his son, simply because he has grown up and developed opinions of his own.

Other minor characters are inserted into the plot for different purposes. Father Buckley and Captain Pasley serve as reminders of home. In addition, the Captain demonstrates that, although we are informed that his family are socially superior to most of the men, he is their 'equal' because they all face the same dangers and the same fate. Similarly, his family are shown to be decent people who, despite their supposed superiority, welcome Willie into their home more warmly than his own relations.

Major Stokes is another example of a contrived minor character. He portrays the arrogant, ignorant British staff officer, who seems to resent the Irishmen under his charge. He is also shown to be cracking under the strain of command, until he eventually chooses to commit suicide. The timing and method of his demise is somewhat incongruous. By the summer of 1918, US troops would have been arriving in substantial numbers, so some relief was at hand. In addition, given the amount of arms and ammunition at his disposal, hanging seems a strange method for him to have chosen.

CRITICAL COMPARISONS

1. DEPICTION OF WAR

Due to the fact that, by definition, the novels of the First World War share many themes and depict similar events, there are ample opportunities to compare the manner and success with which each author has addressed individual occurrences which can often be seen to crop up on more than one occasion.

FEAR

In *A Long Long Way*, Willie's first foray into no man's land fills him with fear, although he appears to quite easily and rapidly put these feelings aside and carry on with his duties. In fact, at various points in the story, we are told that Willie is afraid and yet the only real manifestation of this fear is that he either urinates or defecates. As such it becomes difficult to sympathise with his fear simply because it never changes - the description of it is always the same or very similar. In addition, we never discover the depth of his emotions and he invariably overcomes his terrors quite easily.

Other authors have dealt with this subject, including Remarque in *All Quiet on the Western Front*. Here, however, the author has managed to capture the trembling terror of the trenches and of no man's land in a way which is simply not achieved by Sebastian Barry. Remarque's central character, Paul Bäumer, forms part of a wiring party - in similar circumstances to those of Willie Dunne's first visit into no man's land. A new recruit - although not much younger than Paul himself - looks to him for support and comfort during a bombardment. Paul offers his help to the youngster who is so terrified that he, like Willie Dunne, defecates. Although Barry's use of language in his scenes makes such events understandable and reasonable, Remarque's description is more vivid, because it is more simple, realistic and sympathetically handled. In addition, however, Remarque also uses other means to demonstrate fear throughout the novel and it is this variety which makes the emotion more realistic. It is not enough to simply keep repeating that a character feels fear. His actions must demonstrate that fear, to a greater or lesser extent, dependent upon the circumstances. Remarque does not have to tell his readers that Paul or the other characters in his novel are feeling frightened - that much is obvious by their actions and reactions to the events surrounding them.

DEATH OF FRIENDS

This is another common theme in the literature of the First World War. Willie Dunne's first such experience is the death of Captain Pasley: a good, although inexperienced officer, much respected by his men. Pasley's bravery, although derided by Christie Moran, together with his simple country background make him a figure of hero-worship for Willie who regrets his death and later visits his family as a mark of respect. Again, we are told that Willie misses the Captain and that he is angry and confused about his death and yet we are given no material evidence of these feelings about this death, or the countless others that follow.

In *All Quiet on the Western Front*, Remarque uses a simple device to demonstrate the sense of loss at the death of one's comrades. As each man dies, a single pair of boots is passed on to another man. These boots are handed down from person to person, until there is no-one left to wear them. When it comes to grieving for a particular friend, Remarque's description is brief, simple and effective. One of Paul's particular friends, Stanislaus Katczinsky, known at Kat, dies late in the novel and Remarque gives a short, but very poignant description of Paul's reaction. After Kat's death, Remarque says, Paul simply ceases to be: there is nothing left for him; no hope, no future, no ambition. He has no more left to give.

Similarly, in *Birdsong*, when Stephen Wraysford loses his friend, Michael Weir, he is wracked with guilt that their last words were spoken in anger, but he gradually comes to appreciate how strong his feelings for Weir had become. Wraysford is an emotionally aloof character, greatly affected by his doomed affair with Isabelle Azaire before the war, and he always struggles to express himself properly. After Weir's death, however, he changes. He demonstrably seems to care about other people for the first time since Isabelle left him.

It is hard, therefore, to believe in Willie's Dunne's supposed remorse for the death of Captain Pasley for the very simple reason that they were not shown to be that close in life.

DEATH OF THE ENEMY

Willie Dunne wounds a German soldier during the second gas attack (see Chapter 9) and the man rips off his gas mask, which causes him to die. Later, Willie buries his dead German, having gone through his pockets first. Amongst the man's possessions are a Bible and photographs of his wife and children. Willie spends little time over these items before burying the man, whose memory, we are later told, haunts Willie in his dreams and even at his own death. This implies that the killing of this man is of great significance to Willie and yet the affair itself is rapidly glossed over, which makes its on impact Willie's character seem less credible.

Paul Bäumer has a similar experience in *All Quiet on the Western Front*. He becomes confused and lost in no man's land and, when a bombardment starts, he shelters in a shell hole. Later French troops attack and one falls into Paul's hiding place. Instinctively, Paul stabs the man with his knife but must then remain sheltered with him and watch him die. During the hours of waiting, Paul tries to help the man, giving him water and bandaging his wound. He waits for the man to die, wishing that he could simply shoot him and ease the misery for them both. Eventually the man is dead and Paul, like Willie, goes through his pockets. He discovers the man's name and that he had worked as a printer, plus some photographs of his family. Paul stares at these, promising the dead man that he will take care of his grieving family, send them money perhaps. He realises even as he makes these promises that he does so only to assuage his own feelings of guilt. These discoveries make Paul feel as though he too has been stabbed - through the heart. He dwells for a long time on the impact of the man's death. Remarque's description of Paul's agonised guilt and his insincere promises to compensate the dead man's family show the impact of killing on an individual. Naturally Paul feels extremely guilty and sad, but he later realises that to dwell on this one death is pointless. He has survived and he must go on - and probably kill again. Remarque spends time on this episode, recreating not only the moment of death, but also the consequences.

DESCRIPTIONS OF INJURY AND DEATH

Due to the subject matter of First World War literature, authors must invariably describe scenes of injury and death. In *A Long Long Way*, Barry's language is lyrical in his descriptions: he recounts the sight of Captain Pasley's and the other men's bodies by comparing them with familiar visions, such as old cottage dwellers and devils. He continues in the same style later, when Private Byrne is shot in the eye directly in front of Willie. He compares the wound to a rose bud or a painting, which feels incongruous. The problem with this form of description is that too much is left to the reader's imagination.

The same cannot be said of Sebastian Faulks's *Birdsong*. Here, for example, Stephen Wraysford comes upon a scene of destruction, where several men have been buried in the trench following a shell explosion. Faulks's language is uncompromising as he describes this scene of devastation. Everything is vivid, from the feeling of a wound under Wraysford's fingers, to the smell of fresh blood. One of the survivors - a man named Douglas - has been seriously wounded and Wraysford tries to comfort him as they await the stretcher bearers. He becomes drenched in Douglas's blood and feels that if help does not arrive soon, he will begin to gag on the blood himself. Then, as the stretcher bearers carry Douglas away, another shell strikes and Douglas is tipped off. Wraysford becomes hysterical, screaming at the men to remove Douglas from the trench. This vivid account of the wounds and their aftermath, unlike those in *A Long Long Way*, leaves nothing to the imagination: the reader is left in no doubt about the extent of the wounds or the effect that this episode has on Wraysford. In a later episode some of the men venture out into no man's land to bring back some dead bodies. What they discover is a mass of putrid flesh, which Faulks describes in graphic detail. One of the men, Brennan, finds the decomposing torso of his brother, which he picks up and carries back to the trench. The raw emotion and clear description of the condition of the bodies in this scene is realised by Faulks's use of intense, detailed language.

Equally descriptive is the language of Remarque in *All Quiet on the Western Front*. In chapter 6, for example, he describes an attack in which he recounts the deaths of many men by various means. Like Faulks, Remarque leaves the reader in no doubt as to the nature of fighting and death. There are no comparisons with everyday life, because such niceties have long been forgotten in the desperate urgency to survive.

Reading these three novels, one can see that less lyrical descriptions can sometimes work better, despite their simplicity, because they are just more realistic.

.

BATTLE

In *A Long Long Way*, Sebastian Barry portrays Willie Dunne's participation in several major battles, In each case, however, the descriptions are scant, the action is rushed and Willie Dunne himself seems to be more of an observer than a participant. No man's land is crossed in no time and before we know it, Willie and his comrades are back in their own trenches. Again, Barry's descriptions are lyrical. He tells us in his description of Passchendaele (chapter 18) for example, that many men are losing their heads, or being shot in various parts of their bodies and yet he does not describe this carnage, merely states it as a matter of fact.

Upon turning to *Birdsong*, one can see a similar scene being given a very different treatment. In his description of the first day of the Battle of the Somme, Sebastian Faulks initially builds the tension. The men, including Stephen Wraysford, go into the front line trenches, only to discover that the attack has been postponed by two days. They write letters home, telling of their feelings and their fears. Finally, they go over the top and Faulks gives a vivid description of the scene of battle: the confusion, the injuries, the dead. Again, nothing is left to the imagination as, over the ensuing dozen or more pages, the reader is hurled through no man's land. However, Faulks also manages to make these passages even more realistic by describing the reaction of three observers. Tunnellers Jack Firebrace and Arthur Shaw are joined by the padré, Horrocks, in an elevated position behind the lines. From here they witness the carnage unfolding before them. Horrocks throws away his silver cross and falls to his knees - not in prayer, but in shock. Jack Firebrace turns away, unable to believe what is happening, but also knowing that his faith in God has died. Arthur Shaw simply stands and weeps. Together with the description of the fighting itself, these powerful scenes of regret, torment and pity provide the reader with an infinitely more realistic portrayal of battle.

MALE RELATIONSHIPS

One of the most common themes of First World War literature is the relationships formed between the men who served. In *Birdsong*, although Stephen Wraysford finds it difficult to show emotion following the loss of Isabelle, he clearly becomes very fond of Michael Weir, although he only really appreciates this after Weir's death. Pat Barker's *Regeneration* explores this theme on more than one level. Firstly the friendship between Sassoon and Owen and secondly the fatherly relationship which Dr Rivers shared with some of his patients including Billy Prior. In *Strange Meeting*, Susan Hill exposes a more intense emotional connection between her two central characters. David Barton and John Hilliard meet at the front, become friends and eventually declare their asexual love. The point of their intense friendship is to demonstrate that even the very worst of surroundings can bring out the best in men, making them more tolerant and fulfilled. The novels and plays of the period, written by those who experienced it, also feature this subject. In *All Quiet on the Western Front*, one of the most moving elements is the impact upon Paul Bäumer as each of his friends die. His closest friendship is with Stanislaus Katczinsky (known as Kat) and when his friend is wounded, Paul does not hesitate to carry him back behind the lines to a Casualty Clearing Station. Upon their arrival, Paul is informed that Kat is dead and Remarque's moving description of Paul's reaction to this news reveals the devastating loss he is suffering. In *Journey's End*, R. C. Sherriff examines the aspect of hero-worship as we see former school friends Raleigh and Stanhope adjust to the surroundings of the First World War. At school, Raleigh had always worshipped Stanhope, but now although Raleigh is the new recruit and still eager to please, Stanhope has been in the trenches for so long, he has become war-weary and dependent on alcohol. Through Raleigh's still innocent eyes, we witness the deterioration in Stanhope from the sporting hero of school days to a cynical and yet efficient officer.

Reading through the memoirs of those who served, one is always left with the abiding sense that the one positive aspect which almost every man gained from his First World War experiences were the close bonds of friendship formed during the conflict. This is more common amongst those in the trenches than in the RFC or the Navy or other services, mainly because of their close proximity to one another, shared hardships and the sheer length of time they spent together. In addition, many of those who, like Willie Dunne, enlisted at the beginning of the war, found themselves serving with men they already knew, from similar neighbourhoods and backgrounds, such as in the numerous Pals battalions.

It can be seen, therefore, that this is a realistic, genuine and common aspect of life in the trenches of the First World War and yet it is almost entirely absent in *A Long Long Way*. Willie makes friends easily enough, but these lack the intensity and intimacy to be realistic. Upon a few hours acquaintance, Jesse Kirwan seems to regard Willie as a kindred spirit; Pete O'Hara appears to be Willie's closest friend and yet betrays him on a whim. Christie Moran carries Willie to safety when he has been wounded, but nothing is mentioned of his motive in doing this, so we assume that this is an action which he would have performed for any of his men and therefore this episode tells us more about Christie than his friendship with Willie. By the end of the novel, Willie has spent almost four years in the company of some of these men and yet they seem almost as unfamiliar, both to us and to each other, as on the day the first met. Although many of his comrades die and we are told that this has an effect on Willie, he never really seems to change or to show any affection to those around him. We must be given evidence that the friendships formed at the front are permanent and deep-rooted, and that any loss of such a friendship has a lasting effect. It must be made clear that, without these close attachments, life at the front would have been intolerable; that these bonds were stronger than almost everything else in a man's life. Why? Because that is authentic and such details are what makes these characters real. Without reality they simply cease to matter.

2. CHARACTERS

In the previous chapter, we have provided a critical analysis of some of the characters and how they are portrayed within the novel. In this section, we will compare this with other author's treatment of their characters.

In *A Long Long Way*, Sebastian Barry introduces Willie Dunne as a baby, rapidly passing through his childhood and into the war, which he depicts from 1914 right through to October 1918. The pre-war section of the novel is rushed and this has unfortunate consequences. Willie's actions and reactions become difficult to understand because we cannot fully comprehend his personality, as we know so little about him. This lack of depth to the characters is one of the central flaws in this novel, although many of them feel false and contrived, leading to a lack of credibility throughout.

Other authors - even where the novel is of similar length - spend time on the creation of their characters, using different devices, such as conversations, memories and dreams to fashion plausible characteristics. For example, Paul Bäumer, the central character in Erich Maria Remarque's *All Quiet on the Western Front*, is introduced once he has already been at the front for some time. We learn about his past through his reminiscences and visits home on leave and his conversations with other characters. In addition, because Paul's remembrances are very peresonal to him, we also learn a great deal about his personality. These are the little things in his life which bear great significance such as his feelings towards his family, especially his worries for his mother's health; his hopes for the future; his thoughts about the war. These are not necessarily subjects which he would discuss with his comrades at the front, but it feels as though the reader is being shown Paul's life through an open window - we are observers and yet we are also being drawn in. This treatment enables the reader to focus on Paul during the war, while building an image of his personality as it was before. It also helps to demonstrate how much the war changes him; how embittered and angry he has become and, therefore, how difficult it will be for him to resume his life after the war.

In *Birdsong*, which is a much longer book, Sebastian Faulks spends the whole of the first part of the novel, which some readers find less interesting than the war sections, creating his central character, Stephen Wraysford. Here, he sets the scene of an intense and passionate love affair between Stephen and his host's wife, Isabelle, during the summer of 1910. Stephen, who we quickly learn is a private and somewhat aloof character, reveals details of his past to Isabelle. The effect of this is two-fold: it enables the reader to understand Stephen's childhood and its impact on his personality, but also we learn about how trusting he has become of Isabelle, in that he feels able to speak about such personal thoughts and feelings. This fact becomes even more important when Isabelle leaves him in that we understand how difficult it has been for him to share these thoughts with her in the first place and that by abandoning him she has returned him to utter despair and loneliness.

Both Faulks and Remarque use simple, language to explain the effect of important events on their characters, which makes it easy for the reader to associate with their thoughts. So, when Isabelle leaves Stephen, Faulks says that he 'felt himself grow cold'; Remarque, in describing Paul's reaction to the death of his closest friend, Stanislaus Katczinsky, says simply 'Then I know nothing more.' However, due to the lack of credible personalities in *A Long Long Way*, this simple treatment does not work. When Jesse Kirwan is executed, for example, we are told that Willie knows that 'he couldn't be the same Willie Dunne as he had been before this happened.' But what does this really mean? Jesse Kirwan was a virtual stranger to Willie, so the impact of his death seems unrealistic. More importantly, however, as the novel progresses, these 'changes' in Willie fail to materialise: he simply carries on as before, reacting to, rather than influencing, the events around him.

Other authors make great use of conversation to build their characters. In Susan Hill's *Strange Meeting*, John Hilliard is a reticent, private young man, while David Barton is open and honest and, by gaining Hilliard's trust, Barton enables him to discuss himself and his family. Hilliard's character is initially sketched through his dreams and thoughts while at home convalescing. Barton's is drawn through his letters to his family. It is, however, when the two men come together and begin to care deeply about each other, that we learn even more about them and also about how one person can have such a great influence on another, just by sharing his thoughts, being honest and creating a trusting, lasting friendship.

Pat Barker also uses conversation to great effect in *Regeneration*. Most of her characters undergo treatment with Dr Rivers, for various forms of neurosis and it is during these sessions that the reader gains the most knowledge about each character's personality. In adition, however, Barker also uses conversations between Rivers and, other people, such as Billy Prior's parents which, through their explanations of his childhood, shows the reader even greater detail about his upbringing and some of the reasons behind his difficult temperament. The exposure of flaws in her characters, such as Prior, rather than making them less attractive, actually serves to make them more interesting.

The treatment of female characters - where they feature - within these novels is also worth noting. Gretta Lawlor feels like a contrived and flimsy character: one could even argue that she takes the role of a 'token' female love interest for Willie, since their love affair seems unrealistic. So Gretta's only real contribution to the story is to provide yet another source of unhappiness to hapless Willie Dunne. Her background is vague; the reader can assume that she is relatively independent and that, in accordance with her father's edicts, she 'knows her own mind' and yet she marries another man for no other reason than that he is 'good' and seems to share her own viewpoints and those of her father. One could question whether such an independent girl would really behave in this way, despite the times and the fact that women were not as free as they are today.

Other female characters in First World War literature are often shown to be strong and single-minded. Sarah Lumb in Pat Barker's *Regeneration* is a fairly masculine character who does not easily fall for the charms of Billy Prior and even when he tells her that he loves her, she points out that he really does not have to say such things to her. Sarah provides Billy with a safe haven: someone he can go to in order to escape the war and his memories. Again, Pat Barker has used conversation to demonstrate Sarah's character and Billy's reactions to her. Sarah's conversations with her work-mates show that many of the women with whom she associates are from the same background and share similar perspectives on men and the war. Billy and Sarah also a great deal about many different things, from Billy's role in the war, to Sarah's work and her mother. They frequently disagree with one another, which enables the author to show their characters, their different viewpoints and to develop their relationship more realistically.

In this respect, the association between Willie Dunne and Gretta Lawlor fails. They have been seeing each other for over a year and yet they seem to hardly know one another. Admittedly, their relationship has been carried on in secret, but one could argue that, with Billy Prior being a patient at Craighlockhart Military Hospital, he and Sarah Lumb have, if anything, even less opportunities to become acquainted. Yet this is managed, because Sarah's role in the novel is given due importance by the author. She has an influence on Billy's life and therefore, her character must be adequately developed. Gretta Lawlor, if anything, purports to have a greater impact still on Willie Dunne's life and yet, we know almost nothing about her..

Minor characters, although not as vital as those in the central role are, however, important to the plot.In *A Long Long Way*, Willie is seen to interact with the other characters and, we are told, learns to feel most at home in their company. However, this description lacks credibility as neither he nor the reader really gets to know the other personalities. They discuss issues such as the war, their reasons for enlisting, and the Irish Rebellion, but we still learn little about them or their train of thought. Again, these characters feel strained - as though they have been placed, haphazardly, into the novel to serve a particular, obvious purpose. So, Joe Kielty is there to demonstrate the young man who, having been made to feel intimidated by the giving of a white feather, enlisted in the army and has gone on to become a brave, resourceful soldier; Pete O'Hara is the regular army man, about whose background we learn almost nothing, who demonstrates that betrayal can sometimes be the very worst of all human traits. Equally, Major Stokes is the token foolish staff officer, whose attitude to Willie shows both his own inadequacies and helps to demonstrate Willie's superior integrity. This clumsily demonstrates the theory of the 'Lions led by Donkeys'. Indeed, throughout the novel, officers are portrayed in a less than flattering light. Even Captain Pasley, for all his popularity, is occasionally shown to be lacking in good sense, such as when he stands up in the trench to look out into No Man's Land.

In *All Quiet on the Western Front*, it is the minor characters who actually complete the novel, giving it a realistic roundness. Each man is different, although some of them have been at school together. They have contrasting personalities and gifts: some are more simple, while others could be said to have a bright and shining future ahead, were it not for the war. This exemplifies Remarque's major theme in this novel: that the Great War was, above and beyond everything else, a waste of human lives. Even those who survived, like himself, would never be able to have the same lives they had dreamt of before the war, because nothing could ever be the same again. He shows us this by demonstrating the gradual degradation of his characters from confident, youthful men to cynical, despondent, tired soldiers. Their optimism slowly dies, together with their friends; they become desperate to escape the war - to the point where they will run away and face a court martial for doing so. It is this wearing down of each character, in an individual and personal manner, which makes the whole novel so realistic and poignant.

In many First World War novels, the central character eventually dies. The handling of such events is of great importance as this creates the overriding impression with which a reader is left at the end of the story. Willie Dunne's death comes as no surprise to the reader as his character has already experienced just about everything which life could throw at him, so the only thing left for him now is death. That much is predictable, however, the manner of his death is almost ludicrous. We are told that he dies at the beginning of October 1918 and yet he hears a German soldier singing '*Silent Night*' in the trench opposite, raises his head to sing back and is shot by a sniper. This event feels very contrived. Sebastian Barry uses the carol singing as a means of association with Willie's childhood and the Christmas truce at the beginning of the war, implying that everything which has passed in between has been pointless: we have come full circle but nothing has been achieved in those four years of fighting. Willie's death, like so many others, is therefore seen as being futile. Afterwards, as he lies dying, Willie sees four angels, each representing a significant character in his life. Then Christie Moran and Joe Kielty bury him and mark the grave. Again, this is rushed, so not only do the circumstances of his death seem absurd but the event itself feels remarkably insignificant, especially when compared with this aspect of other First World War novels.

Susan Hill's *Strange Meeting* features the death of one of the two major characters, David Barton. Here, we are actually told almost nothing about the manner of his death. We learn of his family's desperate and fruitless search for information. Most of all, however, we discover about his loss as it impacts upon John Hilliard, the man whom David had loved. Their close and intense friendship had been like nothing else in Hilliard's life and now he must learn to carry on, not only without Barton, but also following the amputation of his leg. His life can never be the same again and Barton's death initially hangs over him like a black cloud. He feels as though he is waiting hopelessly for his life to begin again. Then, however, he decides to visit Barton's family and while travelling to their house, he recognises many of the sights which Barton had earlier described to him.This strange familiarity finally makes Hilliard realise the things which Barton has given him, which had always been lacking from his life before their friendship and which have come to mean more to him than anything else: hope, truth and love.

Billy Prior, the central character in Pat Barker's *Regeneration Trilogy* dies at the end of the final novel - *The Ghost Road*. We can date his death as the 4th November 1918 because we are told that he witnesses Wilfred Owen's demise as he feels his own life slipping away from him. He eventually lies, face down, in the canal, glimpsing his own reflection as he slowly dies. Then, there is nothing but dead bodies, lying in and beside the water as the sun tries to warm their bodies back to life - in a paragraph somewhat reminiscent of Wilfred Owen's poem *Futility*. Pat Barker makes this scene even more poignant still, by contrasting it with an incident at the hospital, where Rivers is treating a man named Hallet who had been serving with Billy Prior and had received a dreadful head injury. Hallet lies on the bed, surrounded by his family and fiancé, crying the incomprehensible statement 'Shotvarfet'. After a while, Rivers comes to understand that what Hallet is actually saying, through his terrible wounds is, 'It's not worth it'. This sentiment is echoed by the other men on the ward, who join in Hallet's cries. Eventually, like Prior, Hallet too dies. Neither death signifies anything: both the hospital ward and the war carry on just as before

In *All Quiet on the Western Front*, the main character, Paul Bäumer also dies right at the very end of the novel. Paul has experienced a great deal during his time at the front, most of his friends are dead and he knows that at home, his family have barely enough food to survive. He has no idea how he will face the future, should he survive the war. Yet in the final chapter, he begins once more to hope. He believes that the war will end soon and, although he feels intensely lonely, he is at least no longer afraid of the future.

At this point, Paul's narrative ends and, until the reader turns the page, one could believe that Paul survives. Remarque then adds a short epilogue, no longer written in the first person, but just a brief description of how Paul met his end. Like Willie Dunne, Paul died in October 1918, with the end of the war in sight. It was a quiet day - hence the title of the novel - and, as he lay dead on the ground, his features portrayed a calm, grateful look - relieved that, for him, the fighting was finally over. This emotive method of ending the novel - raising the reader's hopes and then dashing them - proves very effective. Paul's friends have slowly died around him and the reader has grasped his feelings of hopelessness and begun to wonder what will happen to Paul himself. As his narrative ends, however, there are the first rays of hope as Paul realises that he is still alive and that, whatever else may have happened, he has nothing else to lose and therefore he may as well begin to look forward. The reader feels relieved that here, at least, was one young man who had survived. But no: Remarque crushes our relief, simply by showing us Paul's. Death brings him a release he could never have found in life after the war, which had cost so much and taken from him all his friends, youth, hope and ambitions. Remarque himself had survived the war and one cannot help wondering if he believed that to have lived on was actually the hardest thing of all.

3. LOVE AND SEX

Another fairly common aspect in some First World War novels is the depiction of a love affair. In *A Long Long Way* the central character is evidently deeply in love. Willie Dunne's relationship with Gretta Lawlor lasts for many months before the war and although they are both very young, Willie knows he is in love and twice proposes marriage - offers which Gretta rejects. Barry's description of Gretta is brief and Willie's feelings for her are usually given an air of hopelessness - that eventually, one way or another, this too will be 'taken away from him'. Her feelings for Willie are said to be affectionate and yet there is no real evidence of this. Barry's language in describing them and their relationship is softer and more poetic than in other passages and the physical side of their union is left to the imagination, which contrasts with almost every other description of physical or personal activity, such as the men's toilet habits and Willie's visit to a prostitute, which Barry recounts in infinite and, invariably, basic detail. The effect of this is that Willie's relationship with Gretta takes on an ethereal nature: it lacks tangibility, although this is probably intentional and forms another aspect of the hopeless, unreachable nature of their association.

In Sebastian Faulks's *Birdsong*, on the other hand, the whole of Part One is taken up with building the relationship between Stephen Wraysford and Isabelle Azaire, four years before the war. Theirs is an equally doomed affair, however, as Isabelle is married and although she briefly leaves her husband, it is not long before guilt and anxiety force her back to him. In addition, their affair is given such a depth of passion and intensity that one senses that it could not possibly continue for long: it will have to die because such forceful emotions cannot practically be sustained. Sebastian Faulks leaves nothing to the imagination in describing Stephen and Isabelle's affair: their emotions, as well as their physical unions are fully explained, because theirs is a very demonstrative affair - this is not just sex for the basic need of it, but love fulfilled by sex. Faulks's full descriptions also work because only in this way can the reader hope to realise just how much Stephen has to lose and, ultimately, his utter desolation when Isabelle abandons him. We know and understand why his personality changes from that moment on: we can see why this happens because we can grasp the impact which Isabelle had upon him. Faulks's language in his descriptions of their relationship is, at times, just as basic as that of Sebastian Barry, yet there is greater poignancy here which means that their love is simply more believable.

Pat Barker's *Regeneration* also features her central character, Billy Prior, embarking upon an affair with Sarah Lumb. Billy Prior, however, is a much more complex character than Willie Dunne. His need for sex - rather than love - is based upon the necessity for him to be in control. Prior's experiences at the front have led him to doubt himself, especially his own previously held convictions about manliness, so he seeks to control at least one aspect of his manhood - namely that of sex. For the purposes of the book *Regeneration*, Prior is seen to have a fairly cavalier attitude towards Sarah. He wants to have sex with her, but no more than that and it must always be on his terms. Eventually, however, he falls in love with her - in his own way. Prior is not a man who easily shows emotion or admits to feelings of any type and yet he finds that Sarah Lumb provides him with a feeling of security which he has never experienced before. As such, he loves her. Later, in the second two novels of the trilogy, Prior actively seeks sexual activity of both a homosexual and heterosexual nature. He still loves Sarah and looks forward to spending time with her but his attitude to sex becomes one of necessity, rather than desire. Pat Barker uses coarse language to describe Prior's sexual activity, again leaving absolutely nothing to the imagination. This gives his activities a slightly sordid air, which enhances the reader's perspective of Prior's complex character.

In both *A Long Long Way* and *Birdsong*, the central characters visit a prostitute and one can see similarities in the way in which the authors have described these scenes. Willie Dunne and Pete O'Hara visit prostitutes in Amiens and Sebastian Barry's description of this episode is coarse and yet almost poetic at the same time. This indiscretion on Willie's part, will have far reaching consequences, so an event which may seem insignificant actually becomes rather important within the plot. His motives in this scene, other than the obvious need for sexual relief, are dubious. He is angry with Gretta because she has not written to him and yet if he truly loves her with the passion we are led to believe, can the reader really accept that he would risk his - and Gretta's - happiness? One could argue that he is 'seizing the day'. He has just survived the first gas attack and many of his friends have been killed, so we can believe that he would want to celebrate just being alive. He may not even perceive there being a risk to his happiness - as he might not get caught and Gretta would never know. But he would - and this is where this episode fails to convince. Would this character, who has been shown to be loyal and honest, really take such a chance with his future? Once again, however we have not been given enough information to judge Willie's actions in the context of his character.

In *Birdsong*, Stephen Wraysford takes his virginal friend, Michael Weir, to visit a well-known prostitute at a farmhouse behind the lines. Eventually, although for different reasons, neither man has sex. Sebastian Faulks describes the scene in infinite detail: the effect of the candlelight on the girl's skin as she undresses; Stephen's thoughts as he contemplates her beauty. These thoughts, however, lead him to sad memories of his former lover Isabelle and the moment is lost. This episode shows the reader a great deal about Stephen's personality and the effect of his doomed relationship with Isabelle before the war. We are told that Stephen has not been with a woman for six years and yet not even a basic need for sex can overcome his powerful emotional attachment to the woman he once loved.

Both authors have used very similar descriptions of the women involved. They are described in terms of their beauty; Willie Dunne even fancies that he might be in love; Stephen regards the prostitute in his scene as 'the possibility of love and future generations'. The authors, therefore, romanticise the scene in each case. Sebastian Barry then contrasts this with the description the sex itself, which is hasty and business-like. Faulks, on the other hand, shows the confusion in Wraysford's mind as the girl's flesh - despite its beauty - serves only to remind him not only of Isabelle but also of all the dead and mutilated bodies he has seen on the battlefield. Just looking at these two short scenes in these novels, the reader can quickly see how important character becomes in a story: Willie's actions make little sense, while Wraysford's behaviour - although more bizarre - fits in perfectly with the complexity of his own emotions.

4. LANGUAGE

In *A Long Long Way*, there is no denying that Sebastian Barry's language is expressive and emotional. His description, for example, of Willie's birth right at the very beginning of the novel is packed with metaphors. He recounts the extreme cold; the greyness of both the weather and the buildings of Dublin, the small size of the young baby; the blood which is soon washed away; and how this birth has provided a beacon of hope. The imagery here leaves the reader in no doubt that these were bleak and depressing times, made slightly better by the birth of this child. Barry goes on to give a very brief description of Willie's childhood, the death of his mother and his apprenticeship to Dempsey the builder. We are then introduced to Gretta whose beauty apparently captivates and entrances Willie and yet this description of Gretta's many perfections is juxtaposed with a comment on the unpleasant smell of the pheasants and the squalid details about Gretta's home. This contrast, like the earlier ones surrounding Willie's birth demonstrates that beauty and cruelty can, and often do, easily live side by side.

When Willie enlists, Barry's use of language continues in the same vein. He describes - again very briefly - Willie's journey to the front with his new comrades, telling us that Williams's hair is 'yellow as wall-flowers', and that Clancy's confidence resembles that of a 'robin in winter'. These comparisons with nature remind us that there is still innocence here - although these men have completed some training, war continues to be an awaited experience and they are eager to enjoy their new adventures. Even when they arrive in France, Barry continues to compare their new surroundings with the more familiar sights of home, but then changes in his language begin to creep in. There is a realistic use of profanity in speech, as the recruits familiarise themselves with each other and their new surroundings. Men, such as these, would quite naturally have sworn quite frequently - although that is not to say that this would have applied to all of them: their background and age would have determined their use of language. However, by the end of chapter two, Barry begins to use obscenities within the narrative too. It may have been his intention to contrast the war-time language with that used at home, or simply to show that life - and language - were now universally harsh for these men. However, the real effect of his overly excessive use of profanity, outside of the dialogue is, in fact, to lessen its impact throughout. With so much foul language being used, one no longer feels that these words have any significance whatsoever - they are just words, without meaning or expression. To have continued to use profanity in speech would have been realistic and even necessary: to use it elsewhere merely serves to make it too commonplace, which eventually just detracts from the telling of the story and contrasts too greatly with his more lyrical prose, making the whole novel less convincing.

Most modern authors of First World War literature make use of obscenities in speech - not to do so would simply be unrealistic. However, it would be fairly unusual to find such language within the narrative of most novels. One exception to this would be Pat Barker's *Regeneration* Trilogy, where the language used both in speech and narrative is both coarse and explicit. Despite this, it feels more appropriate than in *A Long Long Way*, in that Barker is, generally speaking, desccribing various sexual acts in an informal manner, appropriate both to the acts themselves and the characters who are participating. The usage of slang terms does not spill over into the general narrative and nor does it become over-used, which means that when such lanague is employed, it feels more appropriate and even necessary.

Novels and plays which were written by those who took part in the war - such as *All Quiet on the Western Front* and *Journey's End*, could not, for reasons of propriety and, of course, censorship, use obscenities at all. They had to convey all of the anger and frustration of soldiering on the Western Front, and yet keep it 'clean' Nonetheless, Remarque's descriptions of battles, wounds, death and hardships are probably amongst the most realistic ever produced. He allows the men and their experiences to speak for themselves, describing their emotions and reactions to the events which surround them. This is a method also employed by R C Sherriff in *Journey's End* and in both cases this is done because neither author wished to simply describe a series of events. Their intention was to show *how* these events changed the people who lived through them .

Throughout *A Long Long Way*, Sebastian Barry's language is ornate and poetic. His descriptions always serve to remind us of Willie's native land, his childhood or memories of home. This provides Willie with a link to home which is clearly important to him; it also serves to remind the reader of the reason why Willie enlisted in the first place - to protect his home (and Gretta) and preserve it for his future. The problem with many of these descriptions is that if the reader has never experienced the sights and sounds of the trenches, but also has no familiarity with the places mentioned in Ireland, such comparisons are of very limited value. So, to be told that the French countryside resembles the fields of Kiltegan is rather pointless, unless one is familiar with one or other scene. This is quite normal - as no author could ever guarantee that his readers would have had such experiences themselves, but ordinarily, an author could overcome this problem by giving his reader a fuller description of the memory to which he is referring. However, Barry's account of Willie's childhood is sketchy at best, which makes it impossible for the reader to visualise his past and form an association between that and his present. This is a shame when one considers that his lyrical language is, therefore, wasted

Other authors make use of symbolic language in their novels. Sebastian Faulks gives time to his descriptions and to creating an atmosphere. So in the pre-war section of *Birdsong*, he creates a heady, passionate, intense mood in the same geographical location as the one where Stephen Wraysford will later fight. In particular, the attention to detail which he offers in his account of a boat trip on the Somme river later forces the reader to compare this scene with that of the battle. The mood of this boat trip is one of intense, pent-up desire between Isabelle and Stephen, but Faulks also introduces a heavier note still, by describing the surroundings in terms of decay. The water is stagnant, the heat oppressive, flies hover above the rotting vegetation. All of this will later come back to the reader when the scene changes to a battleground. Although this link is somewhat obvious, perhaps even a little contrived, it is better to have something realistic and coherent with which to make the comparison and the fullness of these descriptions makes it unnecessary for the reader to have had first-hand experience of the scene.

In *Regeneration*, Pat Barker has employed the language of the poetry from that time. So, in chapter one, for example, she describes Siegfried Sassoon halucinating about men who have 'grey muttering faces' going to face the enemy. This is a direct quotation from Sassoon's poem *Attack*. Other such references appear in various parts of the novel and provide a link between the story and both Owen and Sassoon, who feature in the plot. This adds an air of authenticity, not only to the story as a whole, but also the role of these two poets within the novel.

5. FACTUAL ACCURACY AND REALISM IN A NOVEL

Many people might argue that in a work of fiction, it is not important or even necessary to be realistic or factually accurate. However, when that work of fiction has its basis in historical fact, the author, his editor and publishers have a duty of care to ensure that any facts contained in the novel are accurately represented or are, at least, presented in such general terms that their accuracy becomes less important. This is especially the case when the subject matter is as emotive and easily researched as the First World War. Poor research only leads to factual inaccuracy and that in turn leads to a lack of realism.

The list of acknowledgements at the end of *A Long Long Way* contains ten titles, all of which relate to Ireland's role in the conflict or to the rebellion of Easter 1916. This is understandable, bearing in mind the subject matter of this novel. But there is some evidence to suggest that further general research on the First World War may have been beneficial. This becomes particularly obvious upon reading Chapter fourteen, when Sebastian Barry states that the [front] line ran 'from Portugal to the Sea'. There are two points at issue here. Firstly the Western front never went anywhere near Portugal (although some Portuguese troops were involved in the fighting). Secondly, Portugal *is* on the sea. So, whether one reads this statement from a historical or geographical perspective, it is wrong.

This is one of the most glaring and obvious errors of fact in the novel, but it is by no means unique. Anyone with a genuine interest in the First World War would almost certainly prefer to see generalisations than inaccuracies. So in Chapter 23, for example, rather than stating that America lost over 300,000 troops in a few weeks - which is not the case - Barry may have been better off finding another way of describing the high losses and praising the American's valuable role, which seems to have been his point here.

Other authors have included specific historical or factual elements in their novels, rather than generalising about the war. Pat Barker, for example, in *The Regeneration Trilogy* makes use of historical figures such as Sassoon, Owen, Rivers and Graves, but also uses genuine events woven into the plot of her novels. These include the meeting between Owen and Sassoon, the treatment of shellshock victims and the Pemberton Billing scandal. Pat Barker has included an author's note at the end of each of the novels in the Trilogy and these explain her factual references. Generally speaking, the factual references give the novels an air of authenticity which can help to engage the reader and draw one into the story more effectively. In addition, Pat Barker has 'borrowed' authentic scenes, based in reality, and included them in her novels. For example, the 'eye under the duckboard' incident which led to Billy Prior's breakdown and to him being at Craiglockhart Military Hosptial in the first place, is taken from *Undertones of War,* a memoir by Edmund Blunden, in which the poet describes a very similar incident which happened to him while he was serving at Cambrin in France.

The accuracy of the portrayal of factual elements is vital in capturing the rearder's interest. One cannot remain absorbed in a historical novel once one has begun to doubt its authenticity. Not only is it important to present facts correctly, the author must also make his characters and their exploits realistic and plausible. Here, *A Long Long Way* disappoints for the simple reason that the reader cannot believe in the characters themselves. They are not sufficiently constructed, so one fails to really take any interest in what happens to them. In addition one occasionally doubts the actions or reactions of the characters as genuine. For example, would Major Stokes really have hanged himself? He would have been carrying a revolver, so if determined on suicide, surely that would have been a simpler method. Would one man (Jesse Kirwan) really attempt to strangle another, just because his Bible has fallen into a pot of urine? And would that same man then calmly introduce himself to the very person he had just tried to strangle? Would a German soldier really be singing '*Silent Night*' at the beginning of October, especially bearing in mind that, by this stage of the war, the Germans were retreating and the fighting had become more mobile? Of course, from a literary perspective, this scene provides an ordered ending for Willie Dunne, connecting it with not just his singing ability, but also the Christmas truce. However this incident feels as though it has been invented purely for the purpose of showing the futility of his death. It is, of course, perfectly understandable that the author wishes to portray the pointless nature of yet another death, of yet another innocent young man, but surely there must have been other, better, more realistic ways of achieving this.

This novel also fails to recreate the hardships of battle and of life in the trenches. Sebastian Barry is clearly an author of great ability when it comes to his descriptive language and yet this novel disappoints for the simple reason that it includes too many events and not enough detail. His descriptions of battle fail to involve the reader because they are over too quickly, which makes them feel somehow insignificant. Equally, other aspects of the war could have been given better treatment, such as the extreme cold. The winter of 1916-1917 was desperately cold - the coldest of the whole war, in fact. In Chapter Sixteen, there is a brief description of this winter - which takes up just over a page and hardly does justice to the numbing bitterness of those months. Looking at Wilfred Owen's poem *Exposure*, and reading the letters which he sent to his mother at that time, one can comprehend much better how wretched the men must have felt. His letter to his mother, dated 4th February 1917 describes men who have frozen to death, the wasteland that the countryside has become, and how staring at the unburied, frozen dead in no man's land has sapped his spirits. *Exposure*, which was written with that particular winter in mind, evokes a sense of desolation and hopelessness: that the cold has drained him and his men of every last vestige of hope, to the point where they now have nothing left to give.

All First World War novels, by definition, rely upon an element of realism, both in the facts they portray and the characters who take part and those written from first-hand experience, understandably, tend to be more true-to-life. These authors could, of course, draw on realistic people and experiences and include them within their stories. Remarque's battle descriptions cannot fail to impress; Sherriff's portrayal of the breaking down of the human spirit, as evoked by Stanhope's mental and emotional disintegration, gives *Journey's End* one of its central themes.

There are also modern-day authors who successfully manage to capture the atmosphere and spirit of the time, either by the creation of plausible, interesting characters, or the use of realistic or historically accurate settings, or by giving their whole plot a purpose, distinct from its description of war. Most notable among these is probably Susan Hill in her novel, *Strange Meeting*. Here the element of historical fact and accuracy takes second place to the construction of plausible characters and their reactions to each other and their surroundings. As such, the setting of this novel in the First World War seems almost irrelevant. Barton and Hilliard could have met anywhere. However the fact that the novel is set in the First World War makes their relationship and love all the more poignant. In openly declaring their love, at a time when to do such a thing would have brought disgrace, they are able to demonstrate the journey which they have undertaken together. This is especially true of John Hilliard, whose life has always been devoid of emotional attachments, but who has learned to love and to express his love through his friendship with Barton. To have this love snatched away from them by war adds to the tragedy but it also humanises the conflict in a way seldom achieved with such authenticity.

Historical References

A *Long Long Way* contains references to many historical events around the time of the First World War and there is no shortage of reference material available to those who wish to carry out further research. However, in this section, we have included very brief outlines of some of these events and how they relate to the story, in order to assist students with their understanding of this novel.

THE DUBLIN LOCKOUT

This episode helps to set the scene in Dublin before the war, provides the reason for the meeting between Willie Dunne and Gretta Lawlor and explains some of the differences between their backgrounds.

In 1908, James Larkin established the Irish Transport and General Workers Union (ITGWU), which grew rapidly until, by 1913, it had over 10,000 members. Times were hard for working class families in Ireland: infant mortality rates were high, unemployment levels soared, one third of families in Dublin lived in squalid tenements. Given these conditions, it was relatively easy for Larkin to rally support, when he decided to try and break the anti-union attitude of the Dublin United Tramway Company which was owned by prominent businessman William Martin Murphy.

Murphy was a successful businessman who also owned a department store, a hotel and several newspapers. Although his workers were better paid than many others, their conditions of employment were poor. He saw Larkin as a dangerous opponent and in July 1913, he and 300 other employers agreed to fight the rise of the trade unions. In August, Murphy announced that his employees must denounce the ITGWU or face dismissal. Larkin responded by calling a strike on 26th August 1913, to which Murphy reacted by locking out the workers. Matters escalated further when Larkin organised 'sympathetic' strikes by other workers, which would have a greater impact on Murphy's other companies. The employers then took a collective decision to lock out all workers who belonged to Larkin's union, employing workers from Britain or elsewhere in Ireland instead.

The dispute escalated and violent scenes ensued as strikers tried to prevent the 'blackleg' strikebreakers from entering workplaces. The Dublin Metropolitan Police (DMP) became involved in breaking up the violence. In late August 1913, Larkin appeared at a union rally in Sackville Street. The DMP baton-charged the strikers in an attempt to stop Larkin from speaking and in the ensuing disorder, two civilians were killed and many were injured - on both sides.

The lockout continued until January 1914 when the strikers began to drift back to work. They were virtually starving by this time and accepted the employers' terms. Larkin left Ireland for America and his place was taken by James Connolly, who also took control of the Irish Citizen Army - a worker's militia which he and Larkin had formed during the course of the strike.

THE EASTER RISING

The 1916 Easter Rising plays a crucial part in *A Long Long Way*. Not only do the events themselves feature in Willie's life, but their aftermath is felt throughout the story. Jesse Kirwan becomes disillusioned and actively seeks his own death as a result of the rebellion; Willie's father rejects him because he feels betrayed that his son could even begin to sympathise with the rebels. Also, according to the plot, the way in which the Irish soldiers were treated by the authorities changes as a result of the events in Dublin. The Easter Rising typifies the differences between the opposing sides in Ireland, which stretch back over many centuries.

The English had, for many years, occupied the whole of Ireland, despite the resistance of many of that country's inhabitants and in 1801 the Act of the Union joined Ireland with Great Britain to create the United Kingdom. Irish Catholics were forbidden from entering Parliament and even when Daniel O'Connell managed to have this rule overturned in 1829, little changed, because men usually voted for either their Landlord or his representative, who was, generally speaking, either English or Protestant, or both.

Following the introduction of secret ballots, however, things began to change. A Home Rule party was formed and led by Charles Stuart Parnell. They campaigned for a separate Parliament in Dublin. Over the following years, many

Irish MPs were elected to Westminster and by means of parliamentary obstruction, were able to insist upon having three separate Home Rule Bills introduced, in 1886, 1893 and 1912. These last two Bills were rejected by the House of Lords, but the prime minister, Herbert Asquith, had come to an agreement with the Irish Nationalist leader, John Redmond, that in return for parliamentary support, the Home Rule Bill would become law after 2 years, even if the Lords rejected it. In conjunction with the parliamentary activity, other nationalists were using more direct and sometimes violent means to achieve their aims. The Irish Republican Brotherhood (IRB) had formed as an underground revolutionary body, plotting against the British.

This subject was one upon which Ireland was deeply divided. The Protestant north-east was vehemently opposed to Home Rule and favoured the Union with Great Britain. During 1914, there were many discussions as to whether Ireland should be divided, with the Protestant north remaining under British rule, while the south gained independence. This was not a popular option with the nationalists, who wanted Ireland to be maintained as a whole. It was during these discussions that the First World War began.

John Redmond urged the Nationalists to support Britain in the war, in the belief that Home Rule would be granted at the end of the conflict. The Unionists in the north were also encouraged to enlist as a sign of support for the British and the Union. Thus, men from both the nationalist and unionist sides joined up and fought alongside other allied troops. Not all of the Nationalists agreed with John Redmond - most notably Patrick Pearse, a Dublin lawyer and a leading member of the Irish Republican Brotherhood. Others also disagreed and the IRB joined forces with James Connolly's Irish Citizen Army and the Irish Volunteer Force - which had formed late in 1913. Together these organisations began to plan a rebellion against the British, which included seeking assistance from Germany.

The Rising, which was planned for Easter 1916, necessitated the Volunteer forces taking control of key buildings in Dublin and creating defensive strongholds against any attack from the British army. At noon on Easter Monday, the nationalist troops gathered at strategic points throughout Dublin and began to seize control of a pre-arranged series of buildings, most notably the General Post Office, which became the rebel's headquarters and most of the leaders, including Pearse and Connolly were in that building throughout the rebellion. At approximately 12.45, Pearse stood on the steps of the Post Office and read a carefully prepared Proclamation. In this statement, Pearse declared that, with support from Irish-Americans and European allies, the revolutionaries were seeking to free Ireland from British Rule; that all Irish men and women should be prepared to sacrifice themselves to attain freedom and that the Provisional government would represent the Irish Republic until such time as a properly elected and free government could be formed.

The first attempt by British troops to recapture the rebel territory met with failure as a troop of lancers came under fire from the men in the General Post Office. Although the Nationalists enjoyed this moment of victory, they knew that the British would strike again and, by Monday evening reinforcements of troops had begun arriving from other parts of Ireland, with more on the way from England. The British also used artillery fire and, by Friday, the rebel ringleaders were forced to abandon their headquarters as the building was so badly damaged. Clearly outnumbered and lacking the firepower of the British army, Pearse decided to surrender, rather than risk further loss of life. During the rebellion, 64 rebels, 300 civilians and 130 members of the army and police were killed and there were more than 2,500 wounded on all sides, although the majority of these were civilians.

Although the rebels clearly found some support, there was also a great deal of anger during and immediately after the rebellion, amongst the general population. This situation changed when, on 3rd May, the executions of the ringleaders started and continued for 9 days, when it became clear that public opinion was against such a course of action. Among the 15 men executed were Pearse and Connolly - although the latter was so badly injured that he could not stand to face the firing squad but had to be tied to a chair instead. The eventual outcome was an increase in the popularity of the nationalist movement and a growing anger at the continued involvement of Britain in Ireland.

IRISH SOLDIERS DURING AND AFTER THE FIRST WORLD WAR

The role and participation of Irish soldiers in the First World War forms the basis of this novel. Their nationality becomes even more relevant following the Easter Rising of 1916, after which, many of the characters begin to question their position and also to wonder what will await them at home, should they survive the conflict and return to their homeland.

Although many Irishmen enlisted because of the entreaties of John Redmond and his Unionist counterpart, Edward Carson, who both - for different reasons - urged men to join up and support the British, others had very different motives.

These ranged from a desire to help the people of Belgium, to a need to earn money - and as such, their reasons differed little from the reasons of other men who enlisted. In addition, there were already over 20,000 Irishmen serving in the British regular army and these men formed part of the British Expeditionary Force, which travelled to Belgium in August 1914, taking part in some of the earliest conflicts of the war and in the Christmas Truce.

In 1915, Irish troops took part in the Gallipoli campaign and suffered substantial losses. In May of the same year, the 2nd Royal Dublin Fusiliers were the victims of a gas attack at St Julien, resulting in 645 casualties - out of a force of 666 officers and men. The following April, during the week of the Easter Rising, men of the 16th Irish Division, who had only arrived in France the previous December, were involved in another German gas attack at Hulluch, again resulting in a high percentage of casualties. During the Battle of the Somme, the 36th Ulster Division gained its primary objectives but suffered great losses. Four Victoria Crosses were awarded, but at a cost of 5,500 casualties. Fighting alongside the Ulster-men were the 1st Royal Dublin Fusiliers, and other Irish involvement during this battle included the 1st Royal Irish Rifles, 1st Royal Irish Fusiliers, 1st and 2nd Royal Inniskilling Fusiliers, 2nd Royal Irish Regiment and the 2nd Royal Dublin Fusiliers. Again, many losses were suffered throughout these regiments before the battle finally ended in November 1916.

Th 16th Irish and 36th Ulster Divisions fought together at Messines Ridge in June 1917 and it was during this battle that Willie Redmond MP died. Both divisions also served at Passchendaele which began the following month, under General Gough - who had earned the nickname of 'the mutineer' during the Curragh Incident in 1914. During the Spring Offensive of March 1918, the Irish were, once more, heavily involved, but the losses sustained both here and in the earlier battles were so heavy that many of their replacements had to be found from the English conscripts. Enlistments of Irishmen had dwindled following the Easter Rising and conscription was never introduced in Ireland. These amalgamated and heavily reinforced regiments took part in the final push to drive the Germans into retreat.

Those who survived the conflict returned to an Ireland which had changed drastically over the previous few years. Political differences between Unionists and Nationalists surfaced and the election of December 1918 returned a sweeping endorsement for Sinn Fein, outside of Ulster. 30,000 Irish men died in the First World War and yet the Nationalists preferred to regard these men and the survivors with disdain for having fought alongside the British. The rebels and their followers were now the heroes, while the men who fought and died at the front were all but forgotten.

A QUESTION OF COMPARISONS

Many students have to make direct comparisons between two particular texts, demonstrating the author's treatment of a specific topic. Where this is dealt with as coursework, some examination boards allow that the student may be permitted to choose the texts for themselves. To that end, we have included a list of possible topics and suggested texts which, in our opinion, provide suitable material for such essays, assuming that *A Long Long Way* will be one of the texts involved.

1. EXAMINING THE FUTILITY OF THE WAR

Students who choose to study how futility is portrayed within two texts could look at how the authors have used devices in the plot to convey this theme and how successfully this has been achieved.

USING A LONG LONG WAY AND ALL QUIET ON THE WESTERN FRONT

In *A Long Long Way*, Sebastian Barry has tried, throughout the novel to portray the sense of pointless waste. In his story he is not only referring to the First World War, but also to the conflict in Ireland and it is this clash which helps to further the theme of futility. The men who have gone to fight for the British are seen as having wasted their time - as well as their lives. The Ireland they went to war to protect no longer exists, so what was the point in them going? Barry also uses the repetitive nature of war and battle to further this theme. So, for example, he mentions the Christmas truce at the beginning, and then has Willie Dunne meet his death as the result of hearing a Christmas carol being sung. This event is supposed to demonstrate that, in four years of fighting, nothing has been achieved or gained.

In *All Quiet on the Western Front*, Erich Maria Remarque uses the device of a pair of boots which are passed from soldier to soldier as each man dies. Not only does this show that Paul Bäumer's friends are gradually disappearing around him, but it also demonstrates that eventually the boots will be the only thing left as there will be no-one remaining to wear them. As such, the boots almost seem to take on more importance than the men themselves.

The relative success or failure of these examples lies in their realism. The boots are supposed to be particularly well made and comfortable, which is why each man covets them. On the other hand, the idea of a German, supposedly in the middle of a retreat, sitting in a trench and singing 'Silent Night' at the beginning of October does take a little believing. Barry's use of the Irish conflict to demonstrate this theme is more plausible, but it lacks sufficient detail as to the opinions of the characters to be plausible. Therefore, Barry's treatment would seem to lack credibility and realism.

USING A LONG LONG WAY AND JOURNEY'S END

In both of these pieces, the authors make the point that sometimes the ones who die are the very best of men and that their deaths, quite often, serve no purpose. So, in *A Long Long Way*, Captain Pasley is portrayed as a first-class officer, concerned with the wellbeing of his men and worthy of their affection and respect. Yet, in their very first experience of a gas attack, it is Pasley who dies, acting bravely as befits his personality. This death has a great impact on Willie Dunne, although his knowledge of the Captain has been brief, to the point where Pasley haunts him, even on his deathbed. Nothing is gained by Pasley's death and its result is only suffering, as portrayed in the visit of Willie to the Captain's family.

In *Journey's End*, the theme of futility is best portrayed in the death of Osborne. This character is surely the most likeable and sensible of the officers involved in the play. Married, with two children, Osborne is trusting and friendly - always prepared to put the needs of others ahead of his own. He provides Stanhope with much-needed support, as well as being a father-figure to the younger men in the dugout. His death comes as the result of a raid, which is intended to gain information, but actually provides little or nothing in the way of new facts. Stanhope is bitterly angry at the waste of such an important individual, for no reason. Sherriff shows us the impact of Osborne's passing as following his death, everything changes for those left behind. Raleigh, who had also been on the raid, feels responsible for Osborne's death, while Stanhope has lost the one officer in whom he could place absolute trust.

Again, in order for the effect of the futility of war to be maximised, the author must create a genuine sympathy for the character. Unfortunately, although we are *told* that Pasley is a worthy gentle man, we know so little about him that it is difficult to understand the true impact of his death. The meeting between Willie and Pasley's parents helps in this respect, however, as they are by far the most pleasant and generous people Willie meets, so one can imagine how much the Captain would have meant to them and, therefore, to Willie. Sherriff's creation of characters in *Journey's End*, is more successful - mainly because his piece is a play and one's knowledge of the characters is therefore based on a performance, rather than just on his words. Osborne's loss, demonstrated through the heartfelt despair of Stanhope, allows the reader or audience to glimpse the true effects of such grief on an individual, especially when one can see absolutely no point or value in that person's death.

2. THE EFFECTS OF THE WAR ON THE INDIVIDUAL

The changes which take place in a man's character during the course of war are shown in various ways. Sometimes they become more and more depressed and negative, while on other occasions, they grow more optimistic. Sometimes the effects of warfare are phsical and at other times it becomes a psychological problem. Again, the success or failure of these representations depends almost entirely on their realism.

USING A LONG LONG WAY AND BIRDSONG

Throughout *A Long Long Way*, the reader is told that Willie Dunne is changing. As various events happen around him, especially the events in Ireland and the execution of Jesse Kirwan. The Rebellion makes little sense to Willie, but its impact touches almost every aspect of his life. Jesse Kirwan's death, we are told, makes Willie realise that he can never be the same man again: everything has changed. In addition, being told the sad story of Jesse's childhood haunts Willie like a bad dream.

In *Birdsong*, Stephen Wraysford starts the war as a cynical, depressed character, made bitter by his doomed affair with Isabelle Azaire before the conflict began. The changes which occur in him are the opposite to those which take place in Willie Dunne. This can be seen particularly well in the scene where Wraysford and Jack Firebrace are buried underground. Stephen had previously cared little for his own life, but now, just when it seems to be lost, he begins to long to live.

In both cases, these reactions are normal. The success of the portrayal of Wraysford in *Birdsong*, however, lies in the fact that Sebastian Faulks has taken the time to create a fuller character. This has nothing to do with how likeable a character is, as of the two Willie Dunne is by far the more pleasant man. It is simply that we can understand Wraysford's reactions because we understand him. There are many examples in the texts to show that, while Barry simply *tells* us that Willie Dunne is changing, Faulks *shows* us these reactions, using Stephen's memories of his past and comparing them with his present.

USING A LONG LONG WAY AND REGENERATION

The physical and psychological effect of sustained warfare is often shown in First World War literature. During *A Long Long Way*, Willie undergoes just about every trauma possible. He is forced to kill another man; he is gassed, shot at and comes under shell-fire; his friends die around him, one of them executed by firing squad; his father mocks and abandons him, just because he asks for guidance and dares to show sympathy with the Irish Rebellion; his beloved girlfriend leaves him, marries another man and bears him a child. As such, the effect on Willie should be enormous and it is hardly surprising when, having been wounded in a heavy bombardment, he begins to exhibit signs of shell-shock. In fact it is quite remarkable that he did not show such signs earlier. Barry tells us that he has little control over his head or his left arm and that when he speaks his words are 'thrown about like a baby's food'. Willie is nursed in hospital and during this time, he asks one of the nurses to cuddle him. When she agrees and cradles him like a child, a 'tender miracle' takes place and Willie is cured!

This subject is of great importance in Pat Barker's *Regeneration*, whose title demonstrates that the subject of this novel is the rebuilding of the men who have been thus affected. The patients at Craiglockhart have undergone severe trauma and their symptoms vary greatly. Dr Rivers tries to 'cure' these men, or at least return them to some semblance of normality, by getting them to talk about their experiences. However, during the course of the novel, he also has occasion to visit Dr Yealland and witnesses his, rather different, methods of bringing about a 'cure', which inlcude electric shock treatment. Many of the men who undergo the various treatments will never be the same again. The effects of their trauma have become so deep-rooted in their emotions that they will remain haunted forever. Pat Barker's descriptions of both their symptoms and their reactions to treatment leave the reader in no doubt as to the mental distress through which these men are going.

Although Sebastian Barry only touches on the subject of shell-shock in his novel, his treatment of it is bizarre, especially when compared with Pat Barker's sympathetic and realistic portrayal of the effects of war.

FURTHER READING
RECOMMENDATIONS FOR STUDENTS

Students are often expected to demonstrate a sound knowledge of the texts they are studying and also to enhance this knowledge with extensive reading of other texts within the subject. We have provided on the following pages a list of books, poetry, plays and non-fiction which, in our opinion, provide a good basic understanding of this topic.

NOVELS

STRANGE MEETING by Susan Hill

Strange Meeting is a beautiful and moving book. It is the story of two young men, who meet in the worst circumstances, yet manage to overcome their surroundings and form a deep and lasting friendship. Susan Hill writes so evocatively that the reader is automatically drawn into the lives of these men: the sights, sounds and even smells which they witness are brought to life. It is a book about war and its effects; it is also a story of love, both conventional and 'forbidden'; of human relationships of every variety. This is a tale told during the worst of times, about the best of men.

BIRDSONG by Sebastian Faulks

This novel tells the story of Stephen Wraysford, his destructive pre-war love-affair, his war experiences and, through the eyes of his grand-daughter, the effects of the war on his personality and his generation. A central theme to this story is man's ability to overcome adversity: to rise above his circumstances and survive - no matter what is thrown in his path.

A VERY LONG ENGAGEMENT by Sebastien Japrisot

A story of enduring love and determination. Refusing to believe that her lover can possibly have left her forever, Mathilde decides to search for Manech whom she has been told is missing, presumed dead. She learns from a first-hand witness, that he may not have died, so she sets out on a voyage of discovery - learning not just about his fate, but also a great deal about herself and human nature.

REGENERATION by Pat Barker

This book is, as its title implies, a novel about the rebuilding of men following extreme trauma. Regeneration is a story of man's exploration of his inner being - his mind, feelings and reactions. It details the effects of war on a generation of young men who, because of their experiences, would no longer be able to live ordinary lives.

THE RETURN OF THE SOLDIER by Rebecca West

Written in 1918, this home-front novel gives a useful insight into the trauma of war and societies reactions, as seen through the eyes of three women. Chris Baldry, an officer and husband of Kitty, returns home suffering from shell-shock and amnesia, believing that he is still in a relationship with Margaret Allington - his first love. Kitty, Margaret and Chris's cousin, Jenny, must decide whether to leave Chris in his make-believe world, safe from the war; or whether to 'cure' him and risk his future welfare once he returns to being a soldier.

ALL QUIET ON THE WESTERN FRONT by Erich Maria Remarque

Written from first-hand experience of life in the trenches, this novel is the moving account of the lives of a group of young German soldiers during the First World War. The fact that this, often shocking, story is told from a German perspective demonstrates the universal horrors of the war and the sympathy between men of both sides for others enduring the same hardships as themselves.

POETRY

It is recommended that students read from a wide variety of poets, including female writers. The following anthologies provide good resources for students.

POEMS OF THE FIRST WORLD WAR -
NEVER SUCH INNOCENCE
Edited by Martin Stephen

Probably one of the most comprehensive and accessible anthologies of First World War poetry. The notes which accompany each chapter are not over-long or too complicated and leave the poetry to speak for itself.

LADS: LOVE POETRY OF THE TRENCHES by Martin Taylor

Featuring many lesser-known poets and poems, this anthology approaches the First World War from a different perspective: love. A valuable introduction discusses the emotions of men who, perhaps for the first time, were discovering their own capacity to love their fellow man. This is not an anthology of purely homo-erotic poems, but also features verses by those who had found affection and deep, lasting friendship in the trenches of the First World War.

SCARS UPON MY HEART
Selected by Catherine Reilly

A collection of poems written exclusively by women on the subject of the First World War. Some of the better known female poets are featured here, together with the more obscure, and authors who are not now renowned for their poetry, but for their works in other areas of literature.

UP THE LINE TO DEATH
Edited by Brian Gardner

First published in 1964, this anthology is probably one of the most widely read in this genre. The famous and not-so-famous sit happily together within in these pages of carefully selected poetry.

NON-FICTION

UNDERTONES OF WAR by Edmund Blunden

Edmund Blunden's memoir of his experiences in the First World War is a moving, enlightening and occasionally humorous book, demonstrating above all the intense feelings of respect and comradeship which Blunden found in the trenches.

MEMOIRS OF AN INFANTRY OFFICER by Siegfried Sassoon

Following on from *Memoirs of a Fox-hunting Man*, this book is an autobiographical account of Sassoon's life during the First World War. Sassoon has changed the names of the characters and George Sherston (Sassoon) is not a poet. Sassoon became one of the war's most famous poets and this prose account of his war provides useful background information.
(For a list of the fictional characters and their factual counterparts, see Appendix II of *Siegfried Sassoon* by John Stuart Roberts.)

THE GREAT WAR GENERALS ON THE WESTERN FRONT 1914-1918 by Robin Neillands

Like many others before and since, the cover of this book claims that it will dismiss the old myth that the troops who served in the First World War were badly served by their senior officers. Unlike most of the other books, however, this one is balanced and thought-provoking. Of particular interest within this book is the final chapter which provides an assessment of the main protagonists and their role in the conflict.

THE WESTERN FRONT by Richard Holmes

This is one of many history books about the First World War. Dealing specifically with the Western Front, Richard Holmes looks at the creation of the trench warfare system, supplying men and munitions, major battles and living on the front line.

LETTERS FROM A LOST GENERATION (FIRST WORLD WAR LETTERS OF VERA BRITTAIN AND FOUR FRIENDS)
Edited by Alan Bishop and Mark Bostridge

A remarkable insight into the changes which the First World War caused to a particular set of individuals. In this instance, Vera Brittain lost four important people in her life (two close friends, her fiancé and her brother). The agony this evoked is demonstrated through letters sent between these five characters, which went on to form the basis of Vera Brittain's autobiography *Testament of Youth*.

1914-1918: VOICES AND IMAGES OF THE GREAT WAR
by Lyn MacDonald

One of the most useful 'unofficial' history books available to those studying the First World War. This book tells the story of the soldiers who fought the war through their letters, diary extracts, newspaper reports, poetry and eye-witness accounts.

TO THE LAST MAN: SPRING 1918 by Lyn MacDonald

This is an invaluable book for anyone studying *Journey's End* in particular, as it helps in the understanding of the personalities involved and the time through which they were living. As with all of Lyn MacDonald's excellent books, *To the Last Man* tells its story through the words of the people who were there. It is not restricted to a British perspective, but tells of the first few months of 1918 and their momentous consequences from every angle. The author gives just the right amount of background information of a political and historical nature to keep the reader interested and informed, while leaving the centre-stage to those who really matter... the men themselves.

BIBLIOGRAPHY

A LONG LONG WAY by Sebastian Barry

STRANGE MEETING by Susan Hill

BIRDSONG by Sebastian Faulks

ALL QUIET ON THE WESTERN FRONT by Erich Maria Remarque

THE RETURN OF THE SOLDIER by Rebecca West

JOURNEY'S END by R C Sherriff

REGENERATION by Pat Barker

THE EYE IN THE DOOR by Pat Barker

THE GHOST ROAD by Pat Barker

UNDERTONES OF WAR by Edmund Blunden

CHRONOLOGY OF THE GREAT WAR, 1914-1918 Edited by Lord Edward Gleichen

EASTER 1916 - THE IRISH REBELLION by Charles Townsend

MASTERING MODERN BRITISH HISTORY by Norman Lowe

WEBSITES:

www.bbc.co.uk

www.taoiseach.gov.ie

www.firstworldwar.com

GREAT WAR LITERATURE STUDY GUIDE TITLES

GREAT WAR LITERATURE STUDY GUIDE E-BOOKS:

NOVELS & PLAYS

All Quiet on the Western Front
Birdsong
Journey's End (A-Level or GCSE)
Regeneration
The Eye in the Door
The Ghost Road
A Long Long Way
The First Casualty
Strange Meeting
The Return of the Soldier
The Accrington Pals
Not About Heroes
Oh What a Lovely War

POET BIOGRAPHIES AND POETRY ANALYSIS:

Herbert Asquith
Harold Begbie
John Peale Bishop
Edmund Blunden
Vera Brittain
Rupert Brooke
Thomas Burke
May Wedderburn Cannan

Margaret Postgate Cole
Alice Corbin
E E Cummings
Nancy Cunard
T S Eliot
Eleanor Farjeon
Gilbert Frankau
Robert Frost
Wilfrid Wilson Gibson
Anna Gordon Keown
Robert Graves
Julian Grenfell
Ivor Gurney
Thomas Hardy
Alan P Herbert
Agnes Grozier Herbertson
W N Hodgson
A E Housman
Geoffrey Anketell Studdert Kennedy
Winifred M Letts
Amy Lowell
E A Mackintosh
John McCrae
Charlotte Mew
Edna St Vincent Millay
Ruth Comfort Mitchell
Harriet Monroe
Edith Nesbit
Robert Nichols
Wilfred Owen
Jessie Pope
Ezra Pound
Florence Ripley Mastin
Isaac Rosenberg
Carl Sandburg
Siegfried Sassoon
Alan Seeger
Charles Hamilton Sorley
Wallace Stevens
Sara Teasdale

Edward Wyndham Tennant
Lesbia Thanet
Edward Thomas
Iris Tree
Katharine Tynan Hinkson
Robert Ernest Vernède
Arthur Graeme West

Please note that e-books are only available direct from our Web site at
www.greatwarliterature.co.uk and cannot be purchased through bookshops.

NOTES

NOTES

NOTES

Printed in Great Britain
by Amazon